Bead & Sequin
Embroidery
Stitches

Bead & Sequin EMBROIDERY STITCHES

Stanley Levy

GUILD OF MASTER CRAFTSMAN PUBLICATIONS

First published 2004 by
Guild of Master Craftsman Publications Ltd
Castle Place, 166 High Street,
Lewes, East Sussex BN7 1XU

Reprinted 2004, 2005

Cover and chapter opener photography by Chris Skarbon
Author Photograph by Chris Packham
All other photography by Anthony Bailey

ISBN 1 86108 371 8

A catalogue record for this book is available from
the British Libary.

Production Manager: Hilary MacCallum
Managing Editor: Gerrie Purcell
Commissioning Editor: April McCroskie
Editor: Clare Miller
Book and Cover Design: Fineline Studios

Set in Sabon and Syntax
Colour origination by Icon Reproduction, UK
Printed and bound by Stamford Press, Singapore

Measurements are expressed in metric with imperial equivalents in
brackets, but please note that conversions may have been rounded
to the nearest equivalent. See useful chart on page 117.

Acknowledgements

My thanks to Pam and Ken Bean for their help and time spent going through the book with me.

Kay Kelly, who worked through the exercises.

Hans Neher, without whose computer instructions this book would have taken me a lot longer to complete.

To all the students who pushed me into writing this book in the first place.

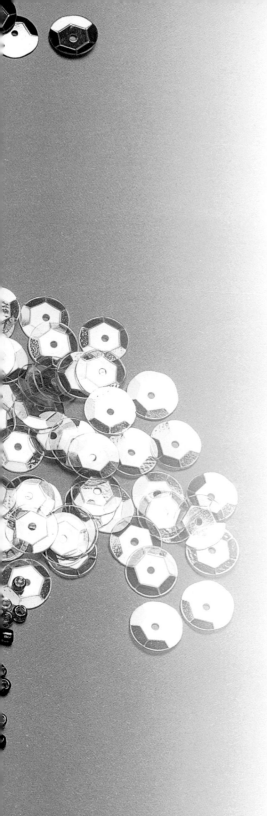

Contents

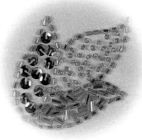

Introduction

This book has taken me many years to complete, and much experience has gone into producing the many examples of work – both my own and my students' – that appear in it.

Over the years I have changed some of my methods and introduced new ones. Some of my early embroideries do not follow the guidelines that I have since developed. The methods I have used and explained may not be the only ones, but they have worked for me. I say to my students, 'First do as I tell you, then do as you like.' I see my book as a guide to the alphabet of bead and sequin embroidery stitches. Learn the alphabet, make your own words, and write your own story.

My designs may be copied, but not those of my students. I hope you enjoy them.

If any errors are found in the book, I would be pleased to be made aware of them, either through the publisher, or my e-mail address, which at the time of going to press is: stancraft@btinternet.com

Chapter One

Getting started

Getting started

The easy-to-follow instructions in this book mean that it will be as useful in the school room as it is to the experienced needleworker. It is written with the intention of showing various sewing methods and applications of beads and sequins for fashion and creative embroidery.

Bead and sequin embroidery, as well as being decorative, can be used to cover stains and stitch marks in garments, as well as for livening up that 'little black dress' or smartening up a tailored jacket. The effects created by beads, and especially sequins, depend on the angles at which they are attached to a surface, the point from which they are viewed, and the influence of lighting and movement.

TIP Make sure you follow each step and understand it before going on to the next one. If you get confused, go back to where you were doing well. Look for any words (refer to the Glossary on pages 114–116), symbols or actions which you may not have fully understood and clarify these before continuing.

TIP Never leave a needle lying about unthreaded. The thread makes it locatable if dropped and easier to remove should it penetrate the body.

Although instructions are given for right-handed people, when they apply to left-handers the change-over will be indicated in brackets. Where necessary, reverse diagrams by looking at them in a mirror or carefully trace over them and reverse the tracing.

Beading needles

The longer and thinner the needle, the more prone it is to bend. Choose the needle to fit the hole in the bead, considering that sometimes the needle has to go through the bead more than once. Never leave a needle lying about unthreaded. The thread makes it locatable if dropped and easier to remove should it penetrate the body. The needles I used were Milwards beading, sizes 10, 11 and 12.

If you prick your finger and get a blood spot on the fabric, chew a corner of a clean white handkerchief or a few metres of white cotton thread rolled up into a ball, until it is thoroughly moistened. Put the blood spot over a piece of clean white fabric and dab the spot with the wet handkerchief or ball. Move the stained fabric to a clean area of the under-fabric and renew the wet handkerchief or ball when necessary. The stain should eventually fade out.

Beads, bugles, sequins and pearls

'Beads' is a general term, taking in all shapes and sizes, but in the exercises 'beads' will refer to embroidery beads. These are usually round, are sometimes slightly flattened and are available in many sizes. Bugles are tube-shaped and come in

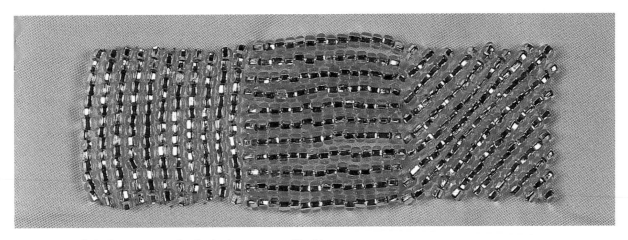

Fig 1.1 Square holes in transparent glass beads give a more sparkly shine

many lengths. They can both have smooth or faceted surfaces and shine differently.

The holes in transparent glass beads and bugles can be square or round, and if silver-lined (or gold-lined, though this is more unusual), will shine differently. The square holes give a sparkly shine (see fig 1.1) compared to the solid shine of the round ones (fig 1.2). Beads can also be lined with opaque colour, but I have never seen bugles coloured this way.

Blackened silver-lined beads can be bleached, making them transparent. Those shown in fig 1.3 have been sewn with red thread, the effect being similar to colour-lined beads. (See 'Care of beaded items', page 17.) Silver-lined beads do not generally seem to be available in pinks or mauves, at the time of writing. – I have yet to find out why. However, they are

available surface-dyed. To check if they are, lay a piece of white fabric in the palm of one hand, place a few beads on it and roll them with a finger of the other hand. The dye will come off. The inside of the hole will also be coloured.

Embroidery beads can be bought pre-packaged, by weight or quantity, or strung in bunches. Many sizes are available, and often there is variation in each size group and the size of the holes. They are made in various materials – glass, plastic, wood and so on – with finishes such as pearl, iridescent (called iris or rainbow), metallic, shiny and matt.

Many sequins, beads, jewellery stones and embroidery pearls come in metric sizes and do not always easily convert into imperial measurements – for instance, 3mm sequins would be almost ⅛in.

Fig 1.2 Round holes have a more solid shine

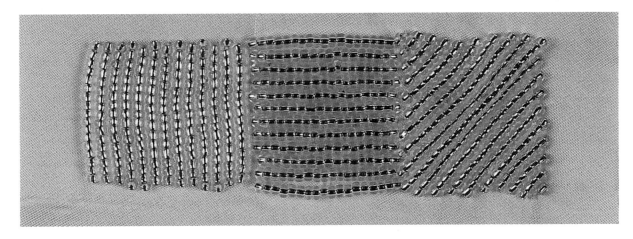

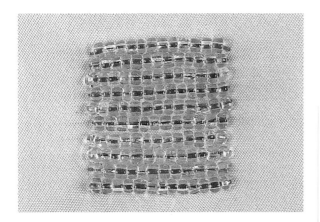

Fig 1.3 Clear beads sewn with red thread

Fig 1.4 Sequins come in a range of shapes, sizes and finishes

Fig 1.5 They can be sold by the 'strip' (left) or 'string' (right)

STRING

STRIP

It is practical, therefore, to have a metric ruler handy, especially when measuring pearls, as stated later in the chapter. Beads may be sold by the gram, 25 grams being about nine tenths of an ounce. Their sizes may vary depending on the manufacturer, but the lower the number, the larger the bead. Size 10, the most popular, are those mainly used in this book. Laid in a row side by side and touching, with the holes facing upwards, ten beads would measure approximately 1.7cm (¾in). Size 7 is a larger bead, measuring 3.5cm (1⅜in).

With bugles, the smaller the number, the smaller the bugle. Ten bugles of size 1 laid end to end would measure about 2.5cm (1in), size 2 would measure 4.7cm (1¾in), size 3 would be 7cm (2¾in) and size 4 would be 9.25cm (3¾in). Larger beads and bugles are also available.

Sequins come in many shapes, sizes, colours and finishes (fig 1.4). They can be transparent with no colour (crystal), transparent coloured, metallic, opaque and with iridescent (rainbow) finishes. The sequin shape which is most popular is round with a centre hole, but there are many variations on this. They can be flat, with an almost indistinguishable rim on the wrong side or they can be cup-shaped and hollow with facets (the hollow side being the right side, though these can also be used the wrong side up, depending on the effect you want to create). They can be bought in packets, by the metre or yard already fixed to a cord (which I call 'strip sequins') which you sew onto the fabric, or by the 'string'

Fig 1.6 Strings of sequins have a 'wrong' side that is less shiny

WRONG   RIGHT

(fig 1.5), which should hold 1000. Be careful to sew these sequins on the correct way, as sometimes the wrong side is not as shiny (fig 1.6). Flat sequins give a more solid shine compared to the sparkly effect caused by cup sequins (fig 1.7). Both these types of sequin can be used for continuous lines, filling in shapes, scattering and rosette motifs. All these techniques will be covered in a later chapter and are used in the exercises in this book.

To check the sizes of round pearls, thread up ten of the same size, measure them against a centimetre ruler and divide by ten to find out the size in millimetres. Ten pearls measuring 3.5cm will be 3.5mm each. Pear-shaped pearls are also available (the holes being either horizontal or vertical), as are oval-shaped beads known as 'oats' (or 'rice' in some countries). These are looked at in more detail in Chapter 5, 'Further techniques'.

Thread

Various threads can be used for bead and sequin stitch work. I prefer mercerized cotton thread for embroidering with beads and sequins, but synthetics can be used. When embroidering with beads or sequins keep the thread not longer than about 40cm (16in) if you are using it single, or 80cm (32in) doubled over. Too long a thread will tangle, and the continual action of the beads sliding along it can cause it to fray and snap. Waxing with beeswax or a piece of white candle helps to prevent this. Use single thread for sequins and double thread for beads on garments or articles in use, though single thread could be used for pictures. As beads are raised off the fabric and could be caught, always start with a knotted thread to make them more secure. Use self-colour thread when sewing beads or sequins, unless a specific colour effect is wanted.

FLAT   CUP

Fig 1.7 Flat sequins give a more solid effect than the sparkly cup sequins

TIP When using mixed colours use thread that works well with all the colours, or that ties in with the background colour.
NOTE This does not necessarily apply to the exercises.

Suggested materials

The following list of materials covers everything you will need to complete all the exercises in this book.

1 x 1000 string of gold (being a useful colour) 5mm cup sequins

2 x 1000 strings 5mm cup sequins, in two other colours of your choice

1 x 1000 string 6mm cup sequins, in a colour of your choice

1 x 1000 string 5mm gold flat sequins

1 x 1000 string 6mm flat sequins, in a colour of your choice

Size 10 beads: 50g topaz, square hole, if possible, 25g topaz, round hole, if possible (change to silver-lined if round and square hole are not available in topaz, or you may not be able to check the difference in shine) 50g each of two other colours

Size 7 beads: 25g in a colour of your choice

Bugles: 50g each of size 1, 2.3 and 4 in topaz or silver

Round pearls: 100 each of sizes 2.5, 3, 3.5, 4, 5 and 6 (you may be able to find an old graduated pearl necklace that can be broken up for this purpose)

Pear-shaped pearls: at least 10 with vertical holes and 10 with horizontal holes

Oval pearls: 100

Thread to match and contrast all colours of beads and sequins

Beading needles sizes 10, 11 and 12

Fig 1.8 Beads, sequins, needles and threads

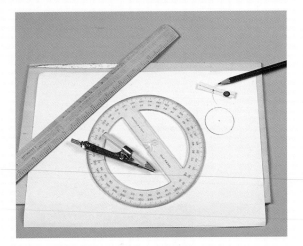

Fig 1.9 Protractor, ruler and compass for designing rosettes

Fig 1.10 Small embroidery frame and adhesive for cut-out motifs

Beeswax

Pencil

Centimetre ruler

Additional pearls for general use (these are cheaper if bought by the 1000)

A few 4 and 6mm jewellery stones (flat-backed ones in metal settings are useful, especially those where the channel holes form a cross). Some embroidery stones and 8mm and 10mm flat and cup sequins would be useful

Dressmakers' carbon paper

Pouncing or tracing powder, powdered cuttlefish, transfer pencil and white chalk pencil are all useful for transferring the designs onto the fabric, see section on designing (Chapter 7)

Protractor and geometry compass for designing rosettes

General sewing equipment (though do not use a thimble, as this would make it harder to pick up beads and sequins)

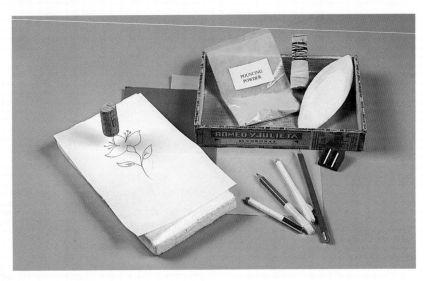

Fig 1.11 Cuttlefish bone, pad and tracing paper in a wood-based box, cork with needle in pattern on polystyrene and various tracing pencils

You will also need a box lid, smooth plastic if possible, or something similar, measuring no less than 10 x 5cm (4 x 2in) and about 1cm (⅜in) deep. This is used to scoop up beads when you need a few beads on the needle at one time. Another shallow lid with a piece of neutral-coloured craft felt stuck firmly inside will help to stop the beads from rolling about too much and makes it easier to pierce the sequins.

Cleaning, washing and ironing

Glass and china beads, pearls, jewellery and embroidery stones, which are 'fake diamonds' and are usually in a metal setting, usually clean and wash quite well. If they are surface-dyed, some or all of the colour will usually be lost. Certain plastic beads and sequins do not take kindly to some cleaning fluids. Some sequins will wash in warm water. Always do a test piece first. Many

theatrical cleaners will have some experience with beaded garments. To iron, lay the beaded side of the garment on clean smooth fabric, such as a sheet, with an underlay of three blankets. Use a warm iron.

Care of beaded items

Colour-lined beads have been known to fade after long periods in strong light. Silver-lined beads and items embroidered with them should not be stored in damp areas or sealed plastic bags in which moisture may be trapped. This causes the silver to turn black and to my knowledge, the initial colour cannot be restored. However, if you do have any loose blackened silver-lined beads, soak them in neat bleach for about 24 hours, shaking them occasionally. Most of the silver will fall away to leave a transparent bead. If any silver remains, thread those beads up, make a few knots in the thread and force the beads over them. You may have to try different thicknesses of thread in order to achieve an effective result. Rinse the beads in clear water and dry in a warm place. These beads can be used for lampshade fringes, and using various coloured threads will give different effects, useful for creative embroidery.

Oil spots

If for any reason you get an oil spot on your fabric, cover the spot with a thick layer of French chalk. If this is not available, scrape a piece of white tailor's chalk over the area so that the powder forms a thick layer. Leave this for a few hours and usually the powder will have taken up the oil and can then be carefully scraped off.

Waxing the thread

Hold a piece of beeswax between the thumb and first finger of the left (right) hand and place the thread end under the thumb, leaving a small piece of thread to hold on to. Then, forcing the thread against the wax with the thumb, draw the thread across the wax with the right (left) hand.

Threading a beading needle

Because the eye of some beading needles is small, a broken thread end will sometimes go through the eye easier than a cut end. Leave the thread on the spool, break off the thread end if it has already been cut, and wax it to a point. Thread the needle using a magnifying glass if necessary.

If you break off the required length before threading the needle and you have difficulty in threading the needle, you may finish up with a shorter thread than you intended. If the needle eye is long, you may find it easier to wax the thread, flatten it between the thumb and first finger, then cut at an angle to make a point. When rethreading a needle, make sure the eye is wax-free by poking a needle point into the blocked eye.

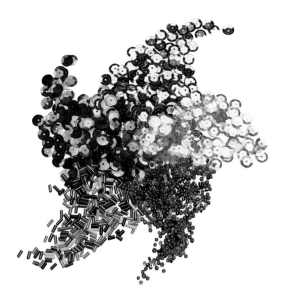

Chapter Two

How to handle
the basic materials

How to handle the basic materials

It is not always necessary or practical to use an embroidery frame, such as when beading a made-up garment, collar, belt or hat. For a picture, however, where it would be stretched before going into a frame, or cut-out motifs, explained in a later chapter, I feel an embroidery frame is necessary. It is important therefore, to be able to pick up beads and sequins using one hand, the other being used to hold the fabric. To follow are some simple guides to picking up different beads and sequins. For these exercises use beading needle size 10, 11 or 12, size 10 beads or 5mm sequins as indicated.

Fig 2.1 Push the needle through the bead and slightly into the felt

Method 1 – to pick up single beads and sequins

Step 1 – Place your beads into a felted container. Hold the needle about halfway along its length, between the thumb and the second finger, the needle point facing the same way as the thumb. Pierce a bead, taking the needle point slightly into the felt (fig 2.1).

Step 2 – Hold the bead on the needle with the forefinger and remove the needle from the felt (fig 2.2).

Fig 2.2 Hold the bead with your forefinger and remove the needle from the felt

Step 3 – Slide the bead to the thumb with the forefinger, take the thumb over the bead, and slide the bead off the needle with the second finger (fig 2.3). This method is also used for sequins.

TIP If you are left-handed, follow the diagrams in a mirror.

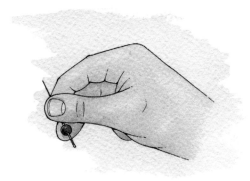

Fig 2.3 Slide the bead off the needle with the second finger

Method 2 – to pick up more than one bead or a sequence of beads and sequins

Pick up a bead as described in Step I of Method I and hold in place on the needle close to the thumb with the forefinger. Keeping the finger in place, pick up another bead or sequin and move the finger to hold this one in place as well (fig 2.4). Continue this action until you have the required number of beads or sequins on the needle, or until the needle is full, then slide them off.

Fig 2.4 Move the forefinger to hold each new bead in place

Method 3 – if the beads come in strung bunches

Take one string of beads and tie a knot over a bead at one end. To stop the bunch from falling apart, put some sticky tape round the ends to keep it together. To pick up a few beads on the needle at one time, place the knotted end of the string of beads in the palm of the left (right) hand, lay the beads at the other end along the forefinger, catching the unknotted string end between the ends of the first and second fingers (fig 2.5).

Holding the needle in the right (left) hand, slide it through the beads from the right (left) and draw them off the string while still holding the beads on the needle. Release the unknotted thread from between the fingers of the right (left) hand while doing this (fig 2.6).

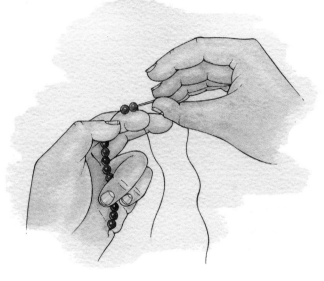

Fig 2.5 Place the knotted end of the string into the palm of the hand and lay the beads at the other end along the forefinger

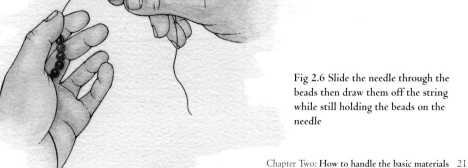

Fig 2.6 Slide the needle through the beads then draw them off the string while still holding the beads on the needle

Method 4 – to pick up many small beads of the same size

To pick up many small beads of one colour or mixed, in no particular sequence, put at least 1.5cm (¾in) depth of beads into an unfelted square or oblong container that is at least 10cm (4in) one way. Holding the needle as before, but nearer the eye, scoop up the beads onto the needle from right (left) to left (right) in the same direction as the length of the container (fig 2.7). Slide the beads off the needle as before. If you haven't the depth of beads, or as they become fewer in the container, tilt it so that the beads pile up.

TIP Some larger beads, or pearls, may need to be picked up singly and placed on the needle. If beads or sequins drop onto the floor, they can be picked up by pressing a damp finger onto them. If they have been scattered on a carpet, scrape them up with a flat piece of wood, such as a ruler, onto a piece of thin card or thick paper.

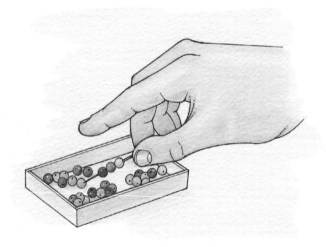

Fig 2.7 Hold the needle near the eye and scoop the beads onto it

Chapter Three

Running stitch –
applications and variations

Basic running stitch

The purpose of the following exercises is to teach the embroiderer the basic running stitch and show its many uses. This stitch can be used for outlining, filling in and making borders.

Abbreviations used in the instructions are as follows:

RS   *right side* of fabric
WS   *wrong side* of fabric
IN   needle through fabric from RS to WS
OUT   needle through fabric from WS to RS
TS and US   *top stitch* and *under stitch*, explained in the running stitch exercises

The basic equipment you will need for the following exercises:

plain light-coloured dress fabric
a beading needle (and an ordinary needle for sequins sewn on their own)
dark thread to show on the light-coloured fabric
a felted container
beeswax or a piece of white candle
scissors, pencil and ruler

You will also need:

approximately 200 each of 5mm or 6mm (approx ¼in) flat and cup sequins of one colour to contrast with the thread
bugle beads, approximately 30 or so of size 3 or 4, of one colour
about 70 of size 10 beads of another colour
a few size 3 or 4 pearls if you have them, to contrast with the thread

●NOTE The stitch names that I use may not relate exactly to other sewing or embroidery stitches.

The colours I have used for the exercises shown are for clarity, not necessarily for artistic effect. Measurements from metric to imperial are approximate. On the fabric, draw three parallel lines about 10cms (4ins) long and 1cm (⅜in) apart. Mark the top line with an even number of dots about ½cm (¼in) apart (fig 3.1). You will not need beads, bugles or sequins for this row.

Thread the needle using double thread that has been waxed and knotted. Hold the fabric in the left (right) hand. Sew from right (left) to left (right). Needle OUT at the first dot, IN at the second – the TS has been made. Needle OUT at the third dot, US made. Continue to the end of the line, finishing with the needle on the WS. The TS holds

•   •   •   •   •   •   •   •   •   •   •

Fig 3.1 Draw three parallel lines on the fabric and mark the top line with an even number of dots

●TIP Using contrasting thread can help you to see any unevenness in the stitch sizes.

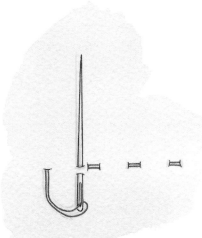

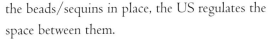

Fig 3.2 Pick up two or three fabric threads with the needle

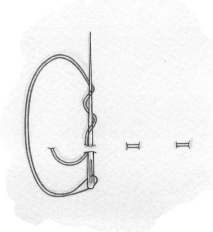

Fig 3.3 Twist the thread around the needle twice before drawing the needle through again

the beads/sequins in place, the US regulates the space between them.

To fasten off, turn the fabric over and about ½cm (¼in) back along the line pick up two or three fabric threads (fig 3.2) and draw the needle through to make a catch stitch. Over this catch stitch make another, but before drawing the needle through, twist the sewing thread around the needle twice (fig 3.3) to make what I call a French knot. After drawing the needle through, make another catch stitch through the knot, pull the thread tight and cut. Always fasten off underneath a bead or sequin so that the fastening-off stitches don't show on the right side.

It is not always necessary to make each TS and US as separate actions. After OUT, put the needle into the fabric where the TS is to be completed and OUT where the next stitch is to start, draw it straight through, completing the TS and making the US in one action. Complete the last stitch by taking the needle through to the WS (fig 3.4).

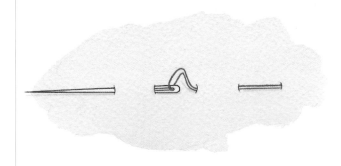

Fig 3.4 The top stitch and under stitch can be made as one action

Running-stitch beads

On the second line (fig 3.5), without using dots, sew a line of bugles. Make sure that the TS is the same size as the bugle. On the third line (fig 3.6), without using dots, sew another row of bugles, making the USs progressively smaller so that at the end of the row the bugles will almost touch

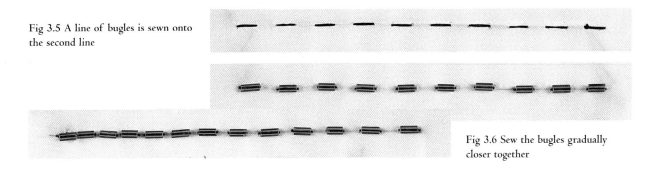

Fig 3.5 A line of bugles is sewn onto the second line

Fig 3.6 Sew the bugles gradually closer together

Fig 3.7 If the top stitches are too short the bugles will bunch

Fig 3.8 Gradually make the spaces between the beads smaller

Fig 3.9 Sew the beads in twos or threes

will always be some space between them). The USs must always be in line with the working line, not at right angles to it. Bunching is caused by the TSs being too short (fig 3.7). TSs that are too long could cause the bugles to move and possibly fray the thread.

Now draw two more lines. On the first (fig 3.8), sew beads singly, spacing them at first and then making the USs smaller. On the second line sew the beads in twos and threes (fig 3.9), making sure the TSs are the same length as the number of beads on the needle. If the TS is too short, the beads will be bunched up (fig 3.10) or raised slightly, which can be done intentionally to create an interesting effect. For variation in texture you can mix bead sizes on the needle (fig 3.11).

By using rows of beads and bugles side by side and by varying the sizes, attractive borders can be built up. When making circles or parts of circles, the tighter the curve, the smaller the bugle has to be.

Fig 3.10 If the top stitch is too short the beads will be bunched up

Fig 3.11 Mix bead sizes on the needle to vary the texture

Running-stitch sequins

Replace the beads and bugles with about 200 flat and 200 cup 5mm or 6mm sequins (all of the same size and colour). Use single thread to contrast with the fabric and sequins for this exercise. Draw ten horizontal parallel lines on the fabric, about 7cms (2¾in) long and a sequin-width apart depending on the size of sequin you are using. Make a small cross at the right-hand (left-hand) side of the top line. Start with flat sequins on the top line at the cross. Needle OUT, put the needle through the wrong side of the sequin, if you can identify it, and slide it onto the fabric. Push the needle through the fabric close to the left (right) edge of the sequin, on the working line (fig 3.12), the TS being half the sequin width.

Bring the needle out further along the line, making the tiniest possible US. Place another flat sequin on the needle and repeat the process (fig 3.13). The second sequin half-covers the first. Continue to the end of the line. If the TSs are too long, the sequins will slide and if too short, they will become bunched up (fig 3.14).

Cover the next four lines the same way. Sew the next five lines with the same-size cup sequins, making sure you put the needle through the domed side so that the hollow side shows when on the fabric. All ten rows must be sewn in the same direction. The flat sequins give a more solid shine

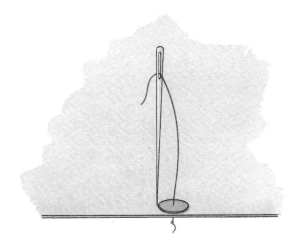

Fig 3.12 The first top-stitch takes in half the sequin

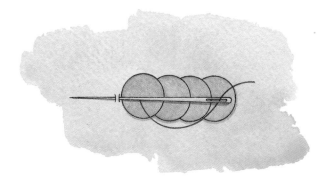

Fig 3.13 Repeat the process with another flat sequin

Fig 3.14 If the top-stitches are too short the sequins will become bunched up and if they are too long the sequins will slide

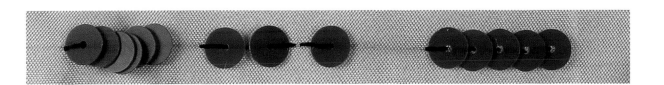

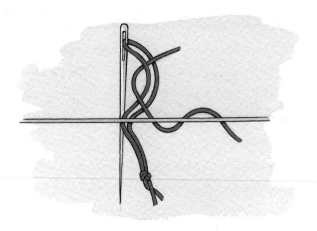

Fig 3.15 When fastening off, the short-cut thread is pushed through the space between the double thread and the needle

Fig 3.16 First put the needle eye through the right side of the sequin, then push the short thread through the space between the double thread and needle

Fig 3.17 Pull the short end through the fabric

compared to the cup ones, which give a more sparkly effect. Hold the fabric against you with the rows going vertically and the cross at the bottom. Look down and see how they shine. Turn the fabric so the cross is at the top; the shine will not now be as strong. When sewing vertical lines, start at the bottom. Sewing rows of sequins in opposite directions gives a striped effect, as will sewing alternate rows of flat and cup sequins.

How to fasten off a short thread

For this exercise, have about 30cm (12in) of single thread in the needle. Make a few running stitches about 1cm (⅜in) long on a piece of fabric, finishing with the needle on the RS. Cut the thread about 8cm (3in) from the fabric. Double the remaining thread and knot the ends together. From the WS, at the spot where the TS is to finish, push the needle eye through the fabric about 2cm (¾in). Push the short-cut thread through the space between the double thread and the needle (fig 3.15).

From the WS, pull the needle and the double thread back out of the fabric, drawing the cut end with it. On the WS, where the short thread is, make a tiny catch-stitch with the double thread and knot the double and single threads together. You can then cut all the threads close or continue sewing if the thread is long enough.

If you need to finish with a sequin on the short thread, put the needle eye through the right side of the sequin (fig 3.16), then push the short thread through the space between the double thread and the needle and pull the needle back out of the sequin, taking the short end with it. Then pull the short end through the fabric (fig 3.17). Beads can be fastened off in this way too.

Running-stitch beads and sequins (A)

You will need 6mm flat sequins of one colour and size 10 beads of a contrasting colour. Use double thread to match the beads. Draw 2 x 10cm (4in) horizontal lines on the fabric 1½cm (⅝in) apart. From the right (left) on the top line, needle OUT, pick up a sequin from the back and two or three beads, enough to cover half the sequin width (fig 3.18). Make the TS the length of the beads. Make a tiny US and continue to the end of the row. The sequins will be raised on the beads behind them.

TIP Because the beads reflect in the sequins, different colour effects can be obtained (see the Plume design, pages 70–71). On the second row, make the USs slightly longer and the beads will show more.

Running-stitch beads and sequins (B)

Use the same materials as for the previous exercise. Draw a line of dots half a sequin width apart. Needle OUT at the first dot, pick up a sequin from the back and enough beads to reach a little further than the second dot. Needle in at the second dot (3.19). The beads will now be slightly raised. Needle OUT at the third dot and repeat. By increasing the number of beads but not the stitch length, a much more raised effect can be created. This method can be used on stretch fabrics, as the stitch will stretch.

Fig 3.18 Pick up a sequin and enough beads to cover half the sequin width

Fig 3.19 Pick up a sequin and enough beads to reach a little further than the second dot

Fig 3.20 Pick up a flat sequin from the wrong side and enough beads to reach the next dot plus two more

Looped running-stitch

Use 6mm flat sequins, 5mm cup sequins and size 10 beads. On a horizontal line make dots 6mm apart, the size of the flat sequins. Starting from the right (left), needle OUT, pick up a flat sequin from the wrong side and enough beads to reach to the next dot, plus two more. Now pick up another flat sequin, this time from the right side. Needle IN at the second dot, needle OUT at the next dot along (fig 3.20). Repeat the process for a few more stitches with varied bead sizes if you prefer. The beads should be raised. For a variation, after the first flat sequin and the first bead, pick up a cup sequin

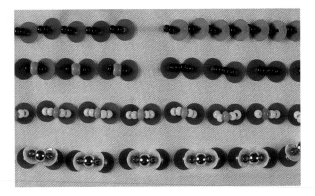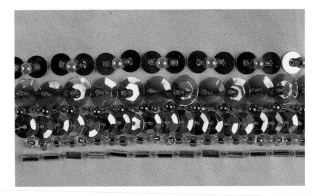

Figs 3.21 and 3.22 A selection of looped running-stitch effects that are attractive when used on borders

from the back, the rest of the beads to make up the number bar one, pick up a cup sequin from the front, the last bead and the flat sequin from the front, and needle IN at the next dot along. Another variation, some of the middle beads can be replaced with a pearl to take up the space. Three or four rows using a 6mm pearl in the centre will give a heavy, chunky effect, suitable for a high-neck collar or the cuff of a long sleeve. All these running stitches sewn side by side in rows can be used to good effect on borders (figs 21 and 22). In fig 3.23, all the rows start at the top, creating the effect seen in fig 3.24.

By sewing rows of sequins in circles that face in different directions (fig 3.25), a spiral effect can be created (fig 3.26). The outer and inside rows start at the bottom, the inner row starts at the top.

Stripes can be formed by sewing rows of the same sequins facing opposite ways (fig 3.27).

TIP Different effects can also be created by sewing sequins to face different ways.

TIP Left-handers may find it easier to look at the diagrams in a mirror.

You can also get an interesting effect by doing this with rows of cup sequins (fig 3.28). Turn the work 180 degrees between each row.

Shading can be created by sewing the sequins so that they face in four different directions (fig 3.29).

Flat and cup sequins sewn in blocks can be used to give a chequered effect over a large area (fig 3.30).

Fig 3.23 Sew sequins from one point in the same direction

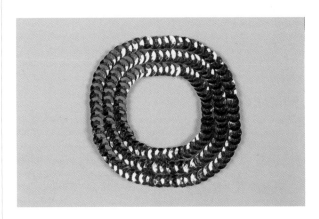

Fig 3.24 Three circles of sequins sewn in the same direction

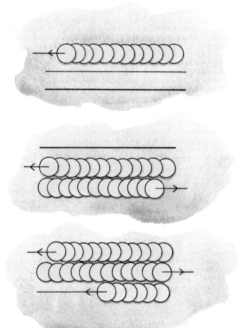

Fig 3.25 Start sewing sequins in circles from different points

Fig 3.26 A spiral effect is achieved by sewing sequins in different directions

Fig 3.27 Sew sequins in opposite directions to create stripes

Fig 3.29 Shading can also be created by sewing the sequins so that they face in four different directions

Fig 3.28 Interesting effects are achieved by sewing rows of cup sequins in alternating directions

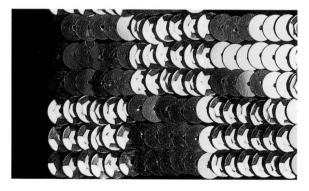

Fig 3.30 Flat and cup sequins can be used to create a chequered effect

Chapter Four

Backstitch –
applications and variations

Backstitch with sequins

Backstitch with sequins makes them overlap more, so that the holes are less obvious. Use 5mm or 6mm flat or cup sequins for this exercise. Draw a horizontal line about 5cm (2in) long on the fabric.

Step 1 – Starting from the right (left), needle OUT a sequin-width's distance from the end of the line (point A). Thread up a sequin from the right side, needle IN half a sequin width to the right (left), (point B). Needle OUT at point C, which is one sequin width from B (fig 4.1). You may need to flick the sequin over so that its right side shows.

Step 2 – Thread up another sequin from the right side, needle IN at point A, which is at the edge of the first sequin, so the first sequin is covered by half. The needle always comes back through to the right side of the fabric half a sequin width away from the previous one (fig 4.2).

Step 3 – Continue this action as in fig 4.3. This backstitch makes a stronger edge than running stitch when used for cut-out motifs, which are explained in Chapter 8.

TIP Left-handers, please note, these diagrams need to be looked at in a mirror.

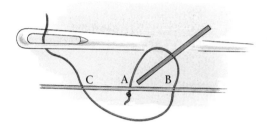

Fig 4.1 Starting the back stitch

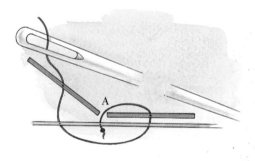

Fig 4.2 Sewing on a second sequin

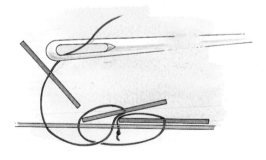

Fig 4.3 Continuing to sew sequins in this way

Backstitch with beads

Use size 10 beads and double thread. As the needle
has to go through some of the beads more than
once, use as fine a needle as possible. The hole in the
last bead you thread up on each stitch will take the
needle twice. Backstitch is ideal if a continuous
unbroken line is wanted.

Draw a horizontal line on the fabric. Work
from left (right) to right (left). Needle OUT on
the start of the line, thread up three beads and
make a three-bead-long TS. Needle IN and bring
it out again on the line behind the last bead and
through that bead again. Thread up two more
beads, make a two-bead-long TS, Needle IN, and
OUT again behind the last bead.

Continue with the last action. When
working on a straight line you can have more
beads on each stitch, but on curves you may need
to keep the stitches small, depending on how
tight the curve is.

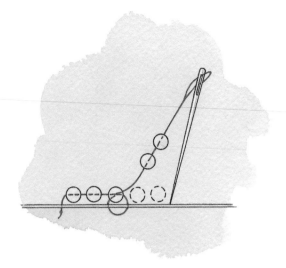

Fig 4.4 After the first three beads, take the needle through the
last bead then thread up two more beads

Fig 4.5 (Below left) The 'fish scale' design can be used to fill an
area and create fish and dragon motifs

Fig 4.6 (Below right) A pearl with beads backstitched around it

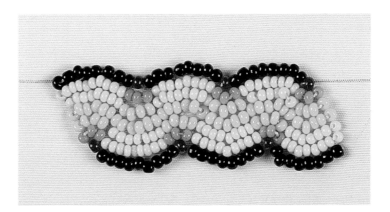

To backstitch around a 6mm pearl, for instance (fig 4.6), estimate how many beads will go around it, pick them up on a separate thread and adjust to fit. To stop being frustrated later, use a size 11 or 12 needle and check to see that the beads will take the needle twice, then remove them from the thread. Sew the pearl onto the fabric. Needle OUT half a bead-width away from the pearl. Thread up four beads, lay them down close to the pearl and bring the needle OUT behind the last bead. Go through that bead again, thread up a few more and again backstitch the last bead you picked up. Repeat this action, and complete the circle by going through the beginning bead.

The 'fish scale' design (fig 4.5) can be used to fill an area, and to create fish and dragon motifs. It is used on the Tree Of Life panel for the 'flower cone' (see pages 92–94).

TIP A flat-backed jewellery stone in a metal setting surrounded by pearls and a pear-shaped pearl drop can look very effective around a neckline, or on the edge of a short sleeve of a wedding dress.

Figures 4.7 and 4.8 Further designs using backstitch with beads

Fig 4.9 Note the angle of the whip stitch

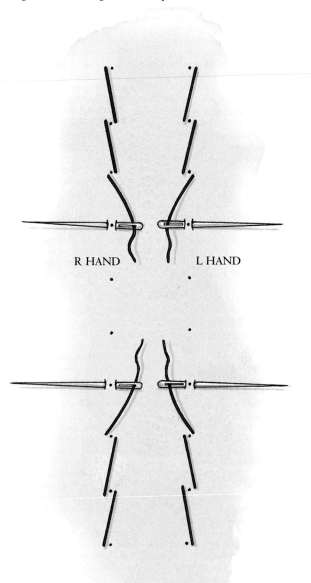

R HAND   L HAND

Fig 4.10 Make several more stitches from the top using the same action, noting that the angle slopes the other way

TIP This stitch can be used for scrolls and stems as well as covering the seams of an empire or princess-line gown. For scrolls, the tighter the curve, the smaller the stitch will need to be.

Whip stitch

For this exercise you will not need beads, just a threaded needle, single or double thread optional, and of course some fabric. Draw a vertical line of 10 dots, the dots being 10mm (⅜in) apart. As it is possible that some of the dots may not be completely covered (when embroidering a garment, for instance) use a vanishing pen or chalk, so that the dots can be erased. Start at the bottom dot (left-handers start from the top). Needle OUT 2mm (¹⁄₁₆in) away to the left (right) of the first dot (when working with beads it will be half a bead-width).

Make a 4mm (⅛in) right-to-left (left-to-right) US under the next dot. First stitch made. Repeat this action, making four stitches in all, finishing with the needle IN the fifth dot. Fasten off. Note the angle of the stitch (fig 4.9).

Now, starting from the top (bottom) using the same action, make four more stitches. The angle slopes

Fig 4.11 An example of the whip stitch with beads

the other way (fig 4.10). It can also be worked on a horizontal line, working from left to right, and right to left to get the angle going the other way, the US being worked vertically from top to bottom. This stitch can be for scrolls and stems as well as covering the seams of an empire or princess-line gown. For scrolls, the tighter the curve, the smaller the stitch must be.

When using beads (fig 4.11) thread up enough to match the stitch length and one more if you want it slightly raised. As a variation, thread up a sequin from the back before threading up the beads. In this instance you will need to experiment with the size of the US to get the effect you want, depending on the size of sequin used.

Fig 4.12 Use an oversew stitch to decorate a folded edge

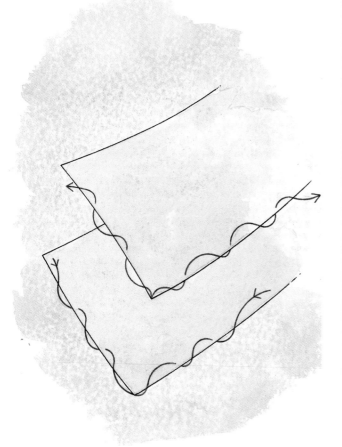

Oversew stitch

Using the same action, oversew a folded edge, such as a collar (fig 4.12). The idea here is to take the needle OUT approximately 5mm ($\frac{3}{16}$in) from the collar edge and OUT again 5mm ($\frac{3}{16}$in) from the edge 10mm ($\frac{3}{8}$in) further along. By increasing the number of beads, the edging will stand more proud. Fasten off the last stitch on the wrong side.

TIP Try using a pearl as the centre bead, or threading up a sequin before the beads as on the collar design, which can also be done with whip stitch. This can also be used as an edging for ornamental pockets, lapels and cuffs on a jacket, as well as a neckline on a wedding or evening gown (fig 4.13).

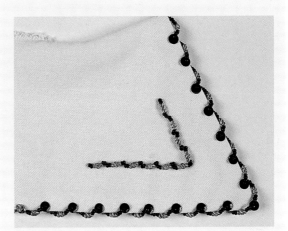

Fig 4.13 This technique makes an effective edging on lapels, cuffs and necklines

Filling-in stitches

There are many ways to fill an area. In the multicolour belt design (Author's gallery, pages 78–79), some areas are filled randomly with bugles, or a combination of bugles and pearls. Other areas are filled with side-by-side rows of bugles executed in backstitch.

The cut-out flower motif (see later chapter), was outlined with sequins, then the outline was followed, row by row, to fill in (fig 4.14). By looking at the photographs you will see the various ways I have used to fill areas. The first photograph (fig 4.15) shows stab stitch, explained later. Fig 4.16 shows backstitch and fig 4.17 is running stitch.

Another technique I use, is to bring the needle out on the outline, thread up a sequin from the back and make the stitch point towards the base of the petal or centre of the flower (fig 4.18). All the outline is done this way. The next row is done the same way, the

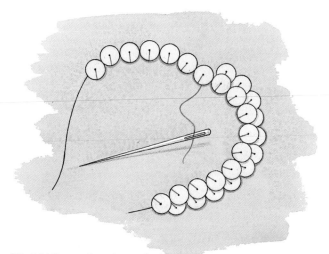

Fig 4.14 Rows of sequins are built up to create a flower motif

needle coming out in line with the inside edge of the sequins of the previous row, so that the stitches of the first row are covered, all stitches pointing towards the centre. For a variation, thread up a sequin and two size 10 beads or a size 2 bugle which will cover the thread. I used this method for the flower effect on the shoulder spray (Author's gallery, pages 80–81). By altering the bead colours you can get a shaded effect, as in the plume design (Author's gallery, pages 70–71).

Fig 4.15 Stab stitch

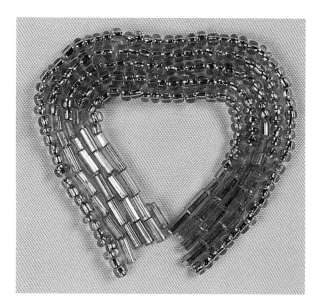

Fig 4.16 backstitch

Fig 4.17 Running stitch

Fig 4.18 Sew lines of sequins with all stitches pointing towards the centre

Satin stitch

This is done with beads or bugles, or a mixture of both. For a leaf, for instance (fig 4.19), needle OUT on the centre vein, thread up enough beads to reach a given point on the main outline, and needle IN. Lay the stitches closely side by side so that no fabric shows between (fig 4.20). Because beads vary in size, you may have to sort out the beads to fit the shape

Fig 4.19 A leaf shape half-filled with satin stitch

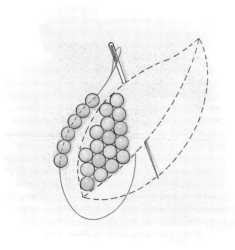

Fig 4.20 Lay the stitches as closely as possible

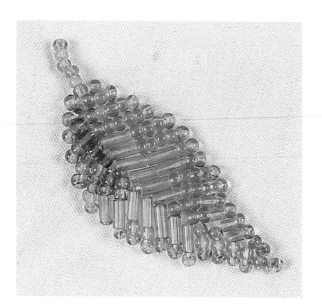

Fig 4.21 Sort the beads to fit the shape

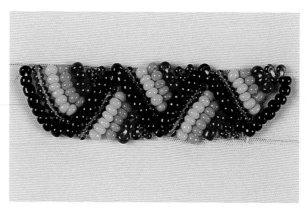

Fig 4.22 Pad satin stitch with rows of beads sewn at right angles to the first row

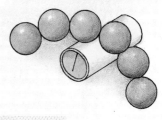

Fig 4.23 To create a more raised effect, sew two or three basic rows side by side before covering them

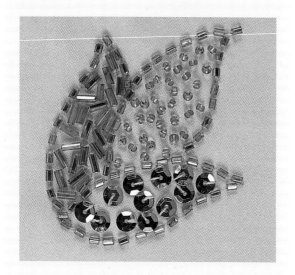

Fig 4.24 'Seeding' – filling areas with randomly spaced beads, bugles or sequins

TIP Another way to fill an area is 'seeding', sewing beads, bugles or sequins, randomly spaced (fig 4.24).

(fig 4.21). I usually start halfway along the leaf on one side of the vein to get the angle as I want it, work to the tip, then work the lower half. Repeat on the other side.

To pad satin stitch, sew a row of beads or a bugle onto the fabric, then sew rows of beads across that row at right angles to it (fig 4.22). For a more raised effect, sew two or three rows side by side before covering them (fig 4.23).

Zigzag running-stitch

This can be used for borders, stripes, curves, made into diamond shapes and elaborated in many ways. It is usually worked between two working lines (as shown in fig 4.25). It can also be used on stretch fabrics. Use size 4 bugles or four size 10 beads for each bugle. To make a pattern for this, if you have a swing-needle sewing machine, by setting the stitch length and width and machining over the pattern paper without thread, you will get the holes, through which you can pounce (see section on pouncing, page 62). For speed on a garment, for instance, with

(see section on pouncing, page 62).

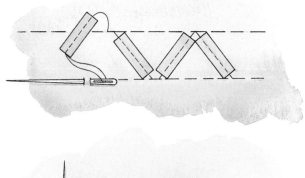

Fig 4.25 The zigzag running stitch is usually worked between two lines

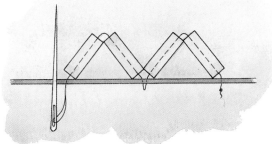

Fig 4.26 To make bugles stand up on a single line, make a one-bugle-length topstitch and a very small understitch

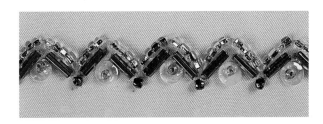

Fig 4.27 Some examples of zigzag running-stitch

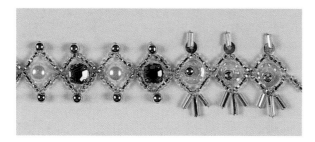

Fig 4.27 Some examples of zigzag running-stitch

Fig 4.28, Standard stab stitch (A) and a raised stab stitch (B)

page 62). For speed on a garment, for instance, with a swing-needle machine, stitch the garment using thread to match the background and then embroider over it. Alternatively, stitch with coloured or metallic-looking thread and then embellish.

Another way is to work on a single line. For instance, starting from the right (left), needle OUT, thread up two size 4 bugles and make a one-and-a-half bugle length TS and a very small US (fig 4.26). The two bugles will stand up. Make a few more stitches like this and fasten off. Starting from the right (left) again, lay each pair of bugles onto the fabric and make a tiny stitch over the thread between them, couching them down.

Stab stitch and stamen stitch

For these exercises you will need 6mm flat and cup sequins, 5mm cup sequins of a different colour, size 10 beads, size 3 or 4 bugles, 3, 4 and 5mm pearls, and double thread to match the beads

To start the stab stitch, draw a row of ten dots, the distance apart to match the 6mm flat sequins you will be using. Needle OUT from one of the dots, thread up a sequin from the back and a bead. Slide the sequin

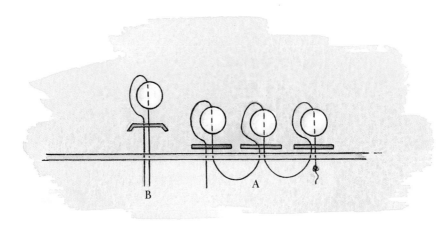

Fig 4.29 Different colour effects in stab stitch

onto the fabric. Take the needle back through the sequin only – the bead holds it in place (fig 4.28, A). If you go back through the bead as well, the sequin will fall off. Sew on two more flat sequins this way. Try four with cup sequins the wrong way up, which will give a more raised look (fig 4.28, B).

Stab stitch can be used for straight and curved lines and can be used to create different colour effects (fig 4.29). The sequins can be sewn closer together so they overlap, and used like this to fill in an area, or they can be scattered. When scattering, it may be necessary to fasten off each one separately if working on a transparent fabric or if the thread on the wrong side could be caught if the garment is unlined.

Now try a different sequence. A 6mm flat sequin from the back, a 5mm cup sequin also from the back and a bead to hold them both in place (fig 4.30, A). Also, try a 6mm flat sequin from the back, a 5mm pearl and a bead (fig 4.30, B). Next, a 5mm pearl, a

Fig 4.30 Alternative sequences in stab stitch

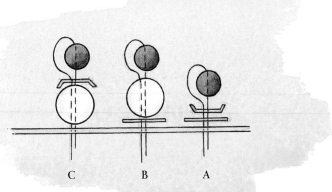

C   B   A

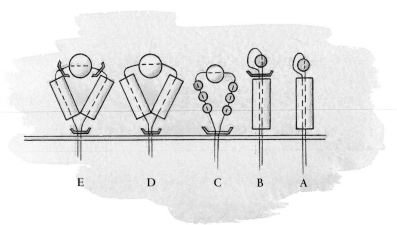

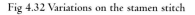

E   D   C   B   A

Fig 4.32 Variations on the stamen stitch

cup sequin picked up from the right side so that it sits on the pearl, and a bead (fig 4.30, C).

As the name implies, stamen stitch can be used to create flower centres (fig 4.31a and b) and is based on stab stitch. These are some sequences you can use.

A bugle with a bead to hold it in place (fig 4.32, A). Next, a bugle, a cup sequin from the back and a bead (fig 4.32, B). For a looped effect, a cup sequin from the back, three beads, a 3 or 4mm pearl and three more beads before going back through the sequin (fig 4.32, C). The beads could be replaced with bugles (fig 4.32, D). Another variation is a cup sequin, bugle, cup sequin from the back, a 3 or 4mm pearl, a cup sequin from the front, a bugle, and back through the first sequin (fig 4.32, E).

Figs 4.31a and b, above and below: some examples of stamen stitches

TIP Stab stitch can be used in a cluster to give the effect of a bunch of berries or grapes. If a coloured transparent sequin is used, the pearl will have a tinted effect. Mix the pearl sizes for a variation.

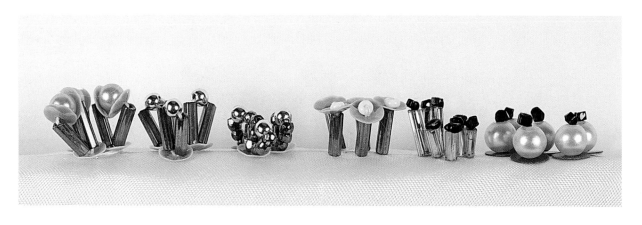

Heather and fern leaf

For this exercise you will need beads and cup sequins. Draw a zigzag line, each line being half the stitch length (see the heavy lines in fig 4.33). Stretch the zigzag towards one end as shown. These lines are for the 'heather'; the main stem can be added later or embroidered first. Needle OUT at point A, thread up enough beads to reach point B, the stitch length, and a cup sequin from the front, or for variation from the back. Needle in at B and OUT halfway back along the stitch, BI, being careful not to displace the beads on line AB. Thread up enough beads to reach C and a sequin, needle IN at C, OUT halfway back, CI. Continue to the end of the pattern (fig 4.34).

The fern leaf can be done just in beads (fig 4.35), but bugles in varying sizes can also be used, depending on the size of the leaf. Space the side stitches according to the effect you want.

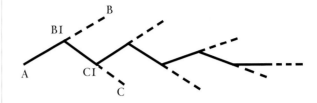

Fig 4.33 Draw a zigzag line for the heather design

Daisy petal

To make a daisy petal (fig 4.36), use size 10 beads. Make a 1cm (about ⅜in) circle of seven or eight equally spaced dots. Needle OUT at any dot. Thread up 12 beads, making sure that the first and seventh beads will take the needle twice. Slide the first bead onto the fabric and take the needle back through it. Lay the loop down so that it radiates from the centre outwards, and stitch down the centre (seventh) bead of the loop. Repeat on the other

Fig 4.34 (Below left) A completed heather motif

Fig 4.35 (Below right) A completed fern leaf

Fig 4.36 (Below) Making a daisy petal

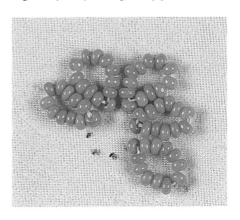

TIP To make a flatter petal, thread up one more bead and stitch down two at the petal end instead of one (fig 4.37).

dots. Fill the centre as you choose. There are many variations and uses for the petal.

To make a pointed petal (fig 4.38), sew the five oval pearls in place first. Needle OUT at the petal point, thread up enough beads to almost reach the centre, Needle IN. The first bead will need to take the needle twice. Take the needle out at the petal end and through the first bead, thread up enough beads to almost reach the centre, needle IN.

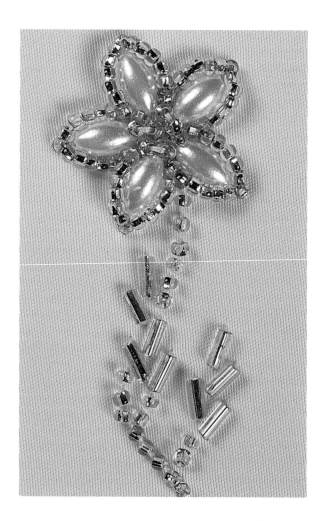

Fig 4.38 A flower with pointed petals

Chapter Five

Further techniques

Looped fringes and tassels

Make a row of nine dots. The space between the first and second is 2½cm (1in), the next space ½cm (⅕in), then 2cm (⅘in), then ½cm (⅕in), then 2cm (⅘in), then ½cm (⅕in), then 2cm (⅘in), then ½cm (⅕in). You will need at least 80cm (31½in) of thread doubled over.

Starting from dot number 1 on the left (right), needle OUT, thread up 5cm of beads to reach dot number 3. Needle IN at 3, OUT at 2. Make another 5cm loop to reach dot 5. Needle IN at 5, OUT at 4, repeat the actions, 4 to 7, 6 to 9, OUT at 8 if you want to continue (fig 5.1a). You could have larger beads at the base of the loop. Try out your own ideas for variations (fig 5.1b and 5.1c).

Make another row of 7 dots 1cm (⅜in) apart. Have the same amount of thread as above. The last bead in every stitch will take the needle twice. Starting at dot number 1 at the left (right), needle OUT, thread up 5cm (2in) of beads. Needle IN at 3, OUT at 2. Thread up 4cm (1⅝in) of beads, IN at dot 4, OUT at 3, needle back through the last bead of the previous stitch, thread up 5cm (2in) of beads minus one bead, IN at dot 5. OUT at 4, needle through the last bead of the connecting stitch, thread up 4cm (1⅝in) of beads less one bead (fig 5.2a). This will give you an attractive alternated loop size, which can be highlighted by using different colours (fig 5.2b).

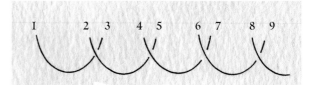

Fig 5.1a A simple looped-fringe pattern

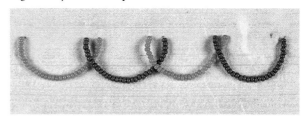

Fig 5.1b Try different sequences of beads

Fig 5.1c Experiment to create a variety of effects

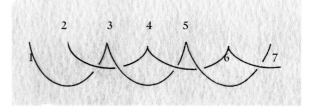

Fig 5.2a A looped sequence with alternating loop sizes

Fig 5.2b Contrasting colours highlight the varying loop sizes

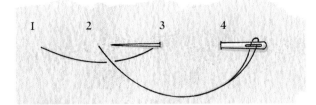

Fig 5.5 The beginning of the cord stitch

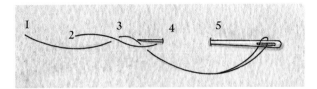

Fig 5.6 Build up the cord stitch with the needle coming out above the stitch

Fig 5.8 Making a three-loop tassel

Cord stitch

This is worked by the same basic method as the looped fringes. Make a row of dots 1cm (⅝in) apart. Number them from left (right) to right (left). Start from the left (right) at dot 1. Thread up enough beads to reach dot 3. Needle IN at 3, OUT at 2 with the needle above the stitch (fig 5.5).

Thread up the same amount of beads, needle IN at dot 4 and OUT at 3, again with the needle coming OUT above the stitch (fig 5.6). If you bring the needle OUT below the stitch, the twist will go the other way. For a variation on the cord effect, alternate the colour on every stitch (fig 5.7). If the different colours are different sizes, match the stitch lengths, not the number of beads. If you want flat ends, it's easier to add half-stitches when the basic cord is finished.

Three-loop tassel

For this exercise you will need a 3mm and a 6mm pearl (or sizes close enough). You will also need enough beads to measure 15cm (6in). Use 60cm (24in) thread doubled over. Needle OUT, thread up the small and large pearls and 10cm (4in) of beads. Take the needle back through the two pearls and fabric. You have now made a large loop (fig 5.8, A). Needle OUT and again through the two pearls. Thread up the remaining 5cm (2in) of beads, pass the needle through the bead at the centre of the large loop (fig 5.8, B) and back through the two pearls and fabric. If you want three different coloured loops, thread up the large loop with 5cm (2in) each of two colours and the last 5cm (2in) with the remaining colour (fig 5.9).

Fig 5.7 Variations on the cord stitch

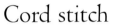

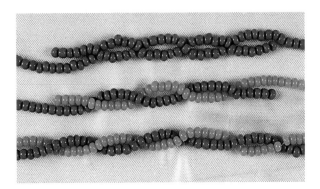

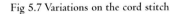

Fig 5.9 Making a three-loop tassel

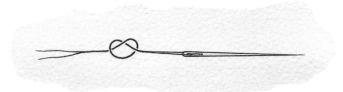

Fig 5.10 Knot the needle onto the thread that you will be using

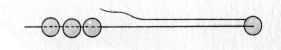

Fig 5.11 Double the thread back after the end bead

Fig 5.12 Make a knot, keeping the end bead in place

Fig 5.13 Slide the other beads over the knot to the end bead

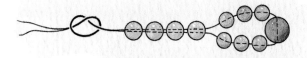

Fringes

Before you start, knot the needle onto the thread that you will be using (fig 5.10). This is to make sure the beads will slide over the knot when you come to fig 5.12.

To make one strand of a 5cm (2in) wide bead fringe, thread up 5cm (2in) of beads on single thread, but do not cut from the reel.

Remove the needle. Slide the end bead to 17cm (6¾in) from the end of the thread, being 12cm (4¾in) longer than the bead's measurement, and double the thread back 17cm (6¾in) (fig 5.11). This allows for sewing onto a ribbon, tape or braid.

Keeping the end bead in place, make a knot 16cm (6¼in) from the bead, taking the bead through the knot (fig 5.12). You can then slide all the other beads over the knot to the end bead (fig 5.13).

If you want to put a larger bead on the end, or a pear-shaped pearl with a horizontal hole, allow two or more beads on either side of it before knotting (fig 5.14).

Fig 5.14 Allow two or more beads on either side of a larger bead before knotting

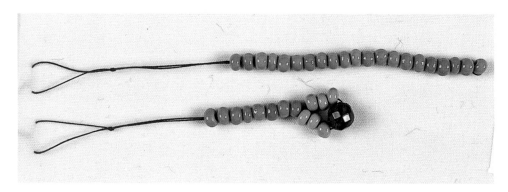

To sew to a tape or braid, cut off the knot. Thread a larger size of needle with the two thread ends. Needle IN the fabric where you want the strand to hang from and fasten off. The advantage of this is that all the sequences that you need can be threaded up at the start for the number of strands or pendants required (somebody else could even do it for you!). Knot each strand sequence individually. When a fancy braid is attached to a garment this is not necessary.

Jewellery stones, embroidery stones and pearls

Jewellery stones are made out of jewel-coloured and mirrored glass in metal settings that are usually silver in colour. If they have faceted backs, the settings are higher, thus standing more proud of the background than those with flat backs, and are more expensive.

TIP This is ideal for a lampshade fringe, where each strand can be fixed to a tape, but make sure the beads are clear so as to allow light to pass through.

These higher settings can be gold- or silver-coloured (fig 5.15). All of these metal settings have holes in so that they can be sewn onto fabric. When sewn on, the thread will hardly show, but being in metal settings it is a good idea to sew them on twice.

Clamping stones, too, have metal settings with claws. The setting is pushed through from the wrong side of the fabric, the claws coming through onto the right side. The stone is placed between the claws, which are then pushed down over the stone to hold it in place.

Fig 5.15 A selection of jewellery and embroidery stones

Embroidery stones are flat-backed mirrored-glass or plastic shapes, also available in jewel colours, either having two holes opposite each other or a central hole, enabling them to be sewn onto fabric. They are available in many shapes including round, square, oval, pear-shape and star. The method of attaching these is either to take the needle up through the hole, thread up a bead, usually to match the stone using matching thread, and thread down again through the hole (but not the bead). Another method is to take the needle through the hole, using matching thread, and down over the side of the stone. Depending on the effect you want, you could also take the needle up through one hole, thread up enough beads to reach to the other one, and down through that hole.

All of these can give a more expensive and glamorous look, but they can also sometimes look overdone, unless on theatrical costumes.

Pearls are available in oval shapes (called oats) and pear shapes as well as round. Those that are pear-shaped can have either a vertical hole going from top to bottom, or a horizontal hole near the pointed end (fig 5.16). These are mostly used for pendants, although those with a vertical hole can be sewn straight onto fabric. If you tried this with those with a horizontal hole, they could twist out of position.

Pendants

To make a pendant, needle OUT, thread up a sequence of beads, pearls, and so on, on double thread with a small bead at the end to hold all the others in place (fig 5.17). Slide them all close to the fabric except the last small bead.

Keeping the thread taut, take the needle back through all the beads, apart from the one on the

Fig 5.16 A selection of pear-shaped and oval pearls

end, and back through the fabric. Don't pull the thread so tight that the pendant won't swing. If you want to put a pearl drop with a horizontal hole at the end of the pendant, thread up, for example, four beads plus five beads before the pearl and four beads after it. Keeping the pearl with four beads on either side of it separate from the rest, take the needle back through all the others, leaving a loop with four beads on either

Fig 5.17 Use double thread to make a pendant

Fig 5.18 Different effects with bead and pearl pendants

Fig 5.19 A & B Two examples of lattice lacing

A

side of the pearl. You can of course use fewer or more beads on either side of the pearl, depending on the effect you want to create (fig 5.18). Be aware that sometimes the needle will go back through the knot and the knot gets pushed away from the fabric.

Lattice lacing

This can look very effective on an evening bag as well as being used in creative embroidery (fig 5.19, A & B). Use graph paper to work out how the basic beads are to be spaced. The different effects depend on the angles at which the basic beads are sewn onto the fabric, and these beads need to take the needle three times.

B

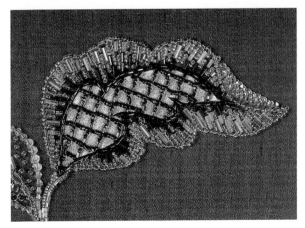

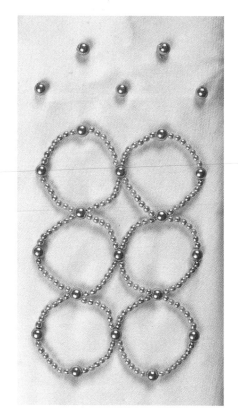

Fig 5.20

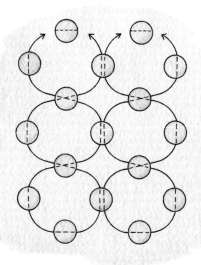

Fig 5.21

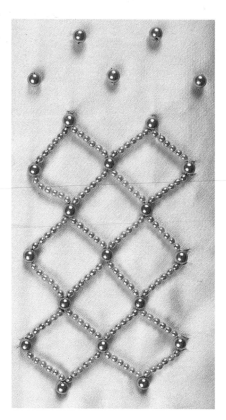

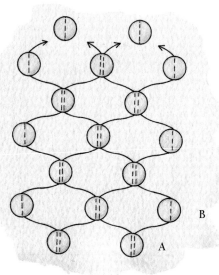

The first lattice (fig 5.20) shows the holes all being vertical. Needle OUT at the base of the bottom bead A and upwards through that bead. Thread up enough small beads to reach the base of bead B, and needle through that bead. Continue 'lacing' the basic beads this way.

The second lattice (fig 5.21) shows beads with the holes on every other row being horizontal.

NOTE Because the lacing beads will most likely not be uniform in size, don't expect to get perfect diamonds or circles.

Chapter Six

Rosette motifs

Rosette motif – making the pattern and the motif

For the first exercise you will need 7 x 6mm flat sequins, 6 x 5mm cup sequins, 18 size 10 beads and one of another colour for the centre. To make a pattern for a six-petal flower, place one flat sequin on a piece of paper and the other six around it, all touching each other. Mark all the sequin centres to give you the outer row of dots and the centre of the circle. To transfer the dots onto the fabric, use carbon paper. Needle OUT at one of the outside dots, thread up a flat sequin from the back, a bead, a cup sequin from the back and two beads. Needle IN 2mm ($\frac{1}{10}$in) from the centre dot. Repeat this action all the way around, and sew the different colour bead in the centre (fig 6.1).

For the second exercise, use 5 x 5mm cup sequins, ten size 10 beads and a 3 or 4mm pearl. A five-petal flower pattern can easily be made by putting one of the sequins on a piece of paper, and around its edge about 2mm ($\frac{1}{10}$in) away mark five dots as equally spaced as possible and also mark the centre of the sequin (fig 6.2). The 'petals' usually overlap each other slightly. Needle OUT at one of the outside dots, thread up a cup sequin from the back and two beads, needle IN 2mm (about $\frac{1}{10}$in) short of the centre. Complete the flower, sew the pearl in the centre. Rosettes can be used to build up borders, scattered over a garment, grouped together to cover a stain, for instance, or made into flower sprays, adding leaves and stems (fig 6.3).

Third exercise. This is less precise. Draw a circle the finished size you would like the motif to be. Around the inside edge place the sequins you want

Fig 6.1 A six-petal flower

Fig 6.2 A pattern for a five-petal flower

to use. If they don't all fit, make the circle larger, or remove one sequin and make the circle smaller (fig 6.4). It is not necessary to have the outside sequins touching. Spaces can be left between them, or the spaces can be filled with beads, smaller sequins or pearls.

Fig 6.3 A&B (Right) Rosettes can be used for all kinds of different reasons

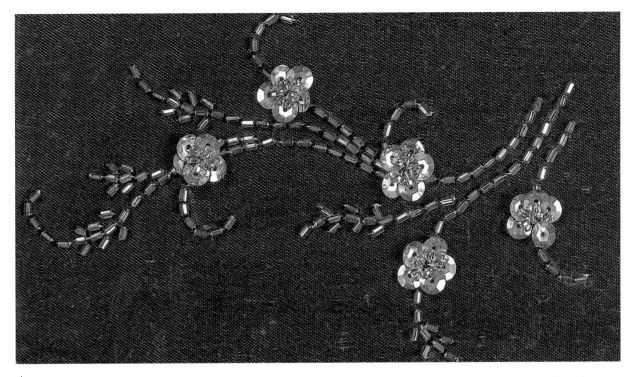

A

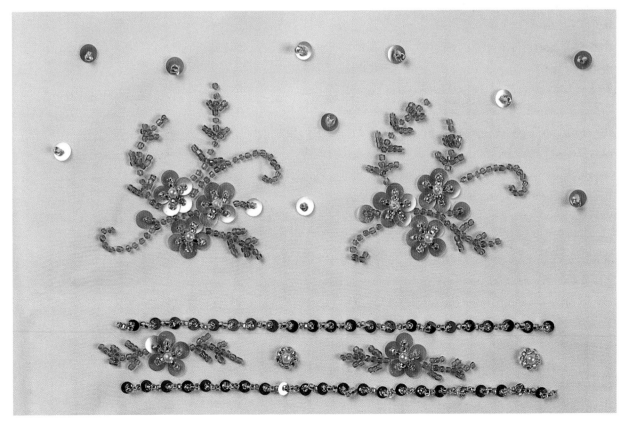

B

Chapter Seven

Designing, pattern-making and transferring

How to transfer designs and patterns onto fabric

If you want to embroider a spray of flowers but don't feel confident about doing it from your own drawing, an effective way of making a pattern is to cut some suitable simple motifs of leaves and flowers, possibly from wallpaper, cards, fabrics or magazines, or cut the rough shapes for them from dark paper. This will make it easier to trace later. Cut out a few shapes of each and arrange the motifs to fit the area they are going to fill. Fix these in place with adhesive tape or other fixative. Cover the pattern with tracing or greaseproof paper and trace over the design, refining the shapes as you do so. Remove the tracing paper and connect the motifs with stems (fig 7.1).

Method A – Using dressmakers' tracing (carbon) paper

This is available in white, yellow, orange and purple, depending on the manufacturer. Place the fabric to be embroidered over a hard smooth surface (but not on your best dining-room table!) Fix the pattern in place with pins or weights. Put the tracing paper carbon side down under the pattern. Do not pin through the tracing paper, as the pin marks will also be transferred. Trace over

Fig 7.1 The three stages of making a flower pattern from rough shapes

the design, being careful not to split the paper pattern. I have been able to use white carbon paper on white fabric. You may need to press hard, so don't use anything with a sharp point in case the pattern splits. A sharp pen or pencil then may mark the fabric. For freehand drawing, try using a white fingernail or chalk pencil. For a small circle, rub the edge of a thimble on tailor's chalk and then press onto the fabric. This is a good method for coloured fabrics.

Method B – Pouncing

The powder used is tracing powder (French chalk), usually obtained in a needlework shop. To make French chalk, scrape tailor's chalk into a saucer or something suitable. Other powder options are powdered cuttlefish or pumice powder. Add powdered charcoal to make grey. Be careful with this as it may stain the fabric.

To prepare the pattern, draw the design on greaseproof paper. If it is a symmetrical one, fold the paper in half. Place it over a sheet of smooth polystyrene (Styrofoam), or many layers of thick fabric, to allow a needle to go through without damaging the supporting surface. Carefully push the eye of a needle into a cork to give you a 'handle', and with the needle point, prick all over the design, making the holes about 2mm ($\frac{1}{16}$in) apart, or stitch over the design with a sewing machine with no thread.

If the design is asymmetrical, draw the pattern in reverse before pricking. This is because when the pattern is placed on the fabric and rubbed over with the powder, the holes do not get closed up. When a symmetrical pattern is opened, one half will be rough because the paper round the holes is raised. When the pattern is rubbed with the powder, the holes on the smooth half tend to

close up a little and the pattern usually isn't quite as well defined.

To trace using this method you will need a pad to take up the powder. To make a pad you can use a 6cm-wide strip of felt cut from a man's felt hat, rolled into a cylinder shape about 3cm (1$\frac{1}{4}$in) diameter. Alternatively, use a strip of sheeting wound around tightly with strong thread to keep it in shape. Trim the ends flat. Put the powder into a cigar box, or onto some other slightly rough surface which will help the pad to take up the powder. Place the fabric on a hard flat surface. Fix the paper pattern on top, rough side up wherever possible, with pins or weights. Rub a flat side of the pad through the powder and then over the design. Lift the pattern off and trace over the design with a dressmaker's chalk pencil on a dark fabric if necessary.

To reverse a pattern, place a sheet of carbon paper on a hard flat surface, carbon side up. Cover this with a sheet of paper and then the pattern. Trace over the design, which will then be transferred to the underside of the sheet of paper.

TIP When transferring a design to a shaped garment such as a fitted bodice, assuming you are making it, you will find it easier to get the design onto the fabric when it is laid flat, before darts are made and the garment is put together. If the garment is already made, you may need to cut the design into sections and transfer the design piece by piece.

Method C – Using a transfer pencil

Draw the design in reverse or go over an existing transfer. Follow the manufacturer's instructions to iron onto the fabric.

Method D – Using a vanishing marking pencil

The design is drawn straight onto the fabric. It should eventually fade out, but read the manufacturer's instructions first.

NOTE I do not recommend using a water-erasable pen for beadwork, as water could damage the embroidery.

TIP For rosettes, you could mark guide dots on small pieces of paper, then pin them where the motifs will be. Embroider over the paper then pull the paper away. Tweezers may be useful for this.

Chapter Eight

Cut-out and small embroidered motifs

Cut-out motifs

I define a cut-out motif as a piece of embroidery cut free from the fabric it is worked on, which can then be attached to another article, such as a garment, belt or other accessory.

It is necessary to work cut-out motifs in a frame, as usually when completed the back is rubbed in with a fabric adhesive that must dry before being cut out. This stops the cut edge from fraying and makes them stiff, especially if you want them to attach to a hat or an evening bag and you want them to stand slightly proud. Another way to make the fabric firm is to iron on a backing-stiffening fabric before doing the embroidery, as sequins will not stand a hot iron.

Small motifs can be used on chokers (fig 8.1), as earrings, fixed to hair clips, shoe clips, or sewn onto narrow shoulder straps on an evening gown.

Motifs can be made by the strip, and a large motif can be used as a brooch (fig 8.2). Motifs on garments can then be swapped for a colour change.

Stretch the fabric in an embroidery frame and draw the design. If you intend to outline with sequins, the motif will be half-a-sequin width larger all around. Use the sequin backstitch as this will give a firmer edge. When you cut out, cut as close to the stitch line as you can. If, for example, you are using red sequins on white fabric and you can see white fabric showing between them, you may be able to get a close colour match with a felt-tip pen, with which you can colour the fabric before spreading the adhesive.

Fig 8.2 A large motif can be used as a brooch

Fig 8.1 Motifs can be used as chokers

Figs 8.3 Scatter motifs

When outlining with beads, keep the shape simple. Use backstitch and do not sew more than about three beads on each stitch, in order to give a strong firm edge. To form a neat edge when cutting out, leave not less than half a centimetre of fabric all around which you can then turn in. A complicated outline would make this difficult. Alternatively, first outline on a swing-needle sewing machine using the colour thread to match the beads, before putting into the frame. Depending on the effect you want, you could outline using a metallic thread in the bobbin, sewing on the wrong side of the fabric, allowing the bobbin stitching to show. You will most likely need to loosen the bobbin spring first.

Small embroidered motifs

These motifs can be used for scattering on a garment, some are also useful for border designs (fig 8.3). Chapter 6, 'Rosette motifs', shows two borders built on motifs. Used repetitively, or combined with other motifs, effective borders can be used for enhancing necklines, edging sleeves, jacket pockets, covering seams, across a bodice or even vertically. You can use these motifs as a basis for your own creations. Some ideas appear in the Students' gallery.

Motifs massed on an evening bodice, including those based on rosettes, can look very complicated. However, they are very easy, if a little tedious, to do. Take a break every so often; it can be tiring on the eyes. Try a few freehand motifs without marking the patterns; they don't have to be perfect! It's the overall effect that is important. Done in iridescent crystal sequins, silver beads and pearls on a wedding dress bodice, with some scattered over the skirt, would please any bride. One advantage of scattering motifs on a large skirt is that once you have marked out where each motif is to be placed, more than one embroiderer can work on it at the same time.

Author's gallery

Starburst

Based on running stitch and stab stitch

The curved lines are silver and blue bugles in varying sizes, the larger bugles being close to the centre. Basic running stitch was used. Stab stitch, single silver 5mm cup sequins held in place with size 10 silver beads were used to break up the lines, and scattered further outwards to enlarge the design. The centre is stamen stitch. Some bugles are topped with a silver sequin, others with an embroidery stone with a central hole. This design can be scattered on a full evening skirt, or adapted for one shoulder of a sleeved evening dress, the lines being extended down the sleeve. It can also be placed across part of the front of a bodice and down the back, on the hip of a sheath evening skirt or as a centrepiece of creative embroidery with a planetary theme.

Silver spray

This template is shown actual size
1 square = 1cm $\left(\frac{3}{8}\,\text{in}\right)$

Plume

Colour-lined beads on silver sequins give the shading effect using bead and sequin running stitch. The plume spray was embroidered from the outside to the base. Starting from the base and working outwards will give a different effect, depending on which way the plume is placed on a garment.

Plume

This template is shown actual size
1 square = 1cm $\left(\frac{3}{8}\text{in}\right)$

Scallop with pattern

The scroll is Running Stitch A, using 5mm cup sequins and size 2 round-hole bugles. The flower stems are whip stitch, size 1 square-hole bugles. For the single stem, size 10 round-hole beads are used; the same beads were used for the rosettes with 5mm cup sequins. 6mm cup sequins and 3mm pearls were used in the side sprays.

This scallop can be used on the edge of an evening jacket, just below the waist on an evening gown, and on the hem. Use your own variations, such as all gold on a wedding gown, or multi-coloured flowers on black.

Scallop with pattern

This template is shown actual size
I square = Icm ($\frac{3}{8}$ in)

Gold rose and leaf

These embroideries show shading effects achieved by
using cup and flat sequins. The rose motif can be
used on a blouse or dress, in the centre of a neckline
or to one side. It can also be used in a creative
embroidery design.

Gold rose and leaf

This template is shown actual size
I square = Icm ($\frac{3}{8}$ in)

Bodice with pattern

Running stitch with beads for the sprays. The pearls
are backstitched. The edge is oversewn.

Move centre dots of side pattern onto the bust
seam. This pattern is for an 81.5cm (32in) bust.
Lengthen or shorten the sprays to fit other sizes
where necessary.

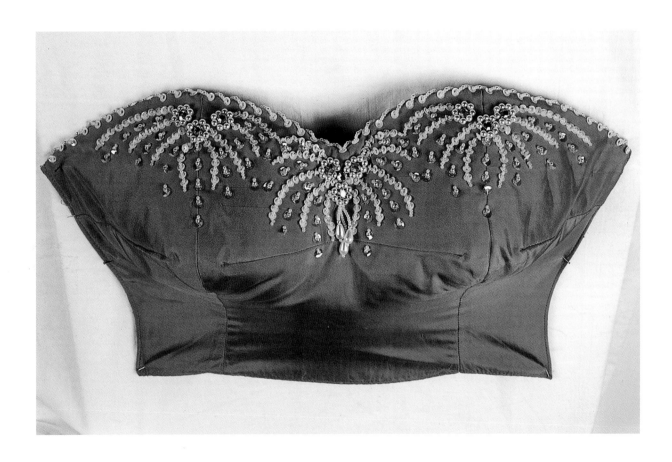

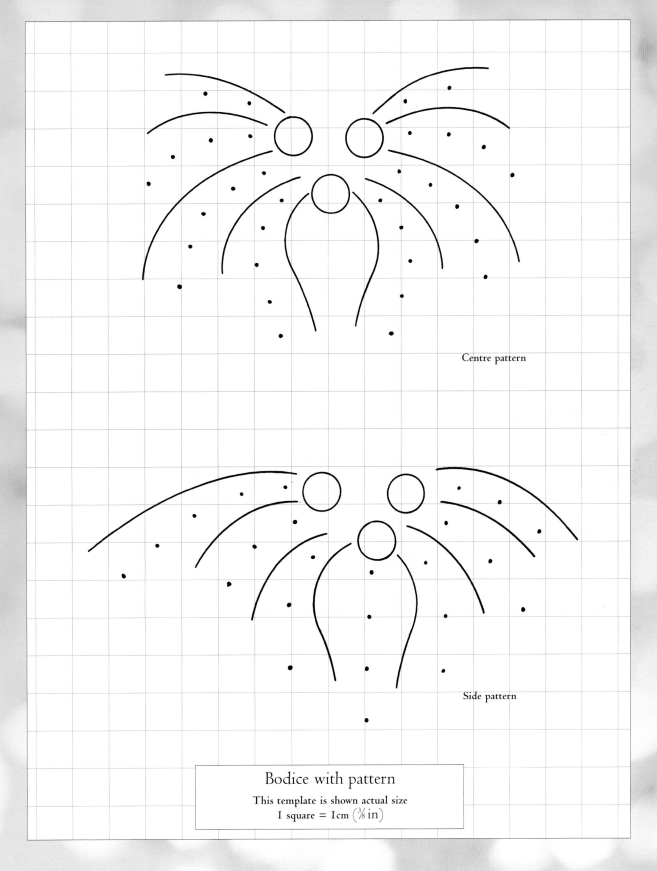

Centre pattern

Side pattern

Bodice with pattern

This template is shown actual size
1 square = 1cm $\left(\frac{3}{8}\text{in}\right)$

Belt

The silver bugle lines are basic running stitch. The motif outlines are two rows of backstitch using size 10 beads. Bugles have been used to separate the areas, which are filled with random fillings that you can design yourself. Bead oddments and pearls from old or broken necklaces could be very useful. This design can be used on a belt, waistline, as a spray at an angle on a bodice top, and as a square neckline motif.

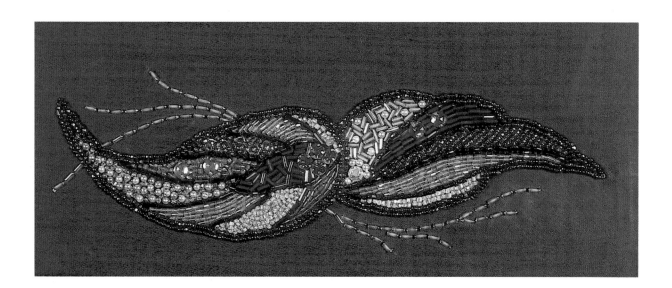

Belt

This template is shown actual size
1 square = 1cm $\left(\frac{3}{8} \text{in}\right)$

Shoulder spray with pattern

Outline in running stitch, backstitch filling.

Shoulder spray with pattern

This template is shown actual size

I square = 1cm $\left(\frac{3}{8}\text{in}\right)$

Silver spray

Silver bugles in running stitch outline the leaves.
The flower motifs are running stitch with silver cup
sequins, radiation filling using irridescent sequins
and beads. Looped running stitch topped with
pearls completes the centre.

Silver spray

This template is shown actual size
1 square = 1cm ($\frac{3}{8}$ in)

Cut-out motifs

Cut-out motifs arranged into a spray, useful for
the shoulder of a bodice. Fewer motifs could be
arranged on an evening bag, more could be arranged
around a neckline or on shoulder straps. Smaller
motifs fitted onto shoe clips could be worn for
evening wear. Copy these motifs or design your
own shapes.

Cut-out motif

This template is shown actual size
1 square = 1cm ($\frac{3}{8}$ in)

Cut-out motif

This template is shown actual size
I square = Icm ($\frac{3}{8}$ in)

Cut-out motifs

These templates are shown actual size
1 square = 1cm ($\frac{3}{8}$in)

Hem scroll with pattern

Stitches used: mostly running stitch with beads and
sequins, but also heather, stab and whip, including
a tassel.

Hem scroll with pattern

This template is shown actual size
I square = Icm ($\frac{3}{8}$in)

Heart with pattern

Here showing effects of couched flat-strip sequins
and cup sequins in running stitch, with variations.

Heart with pattern

This template is shown actual size
I square = Icm ($\frac{3}{8}$ in)

Tree of life panel

70.5cm (27in) x 48cm (19in)

Tree of life close-ups

Evening jacket

Low-back velvet dress

Designs suitable for a low-back velvet dress

This template is shown actual size
I square = Icm $\left(\frac{3}{8}\text{in}\right)$

Students' gallery

Fire-screen panel – Pam Bean

The design was taken from a carved wood panel.

Fritillaries and thistle – Carolyn Last

Butterfly collar – Joy Way

Fantasy bird – Joy Way

The forewing was made as a separate cut-out and
later attached to make a three-dimensional picture.

Blue velvet handbag – Joy McGill

Evening jacket motifs – Louise Jourdain

The motifs were used to edge the fronts, pockets
and sleeves of the evening jacket.

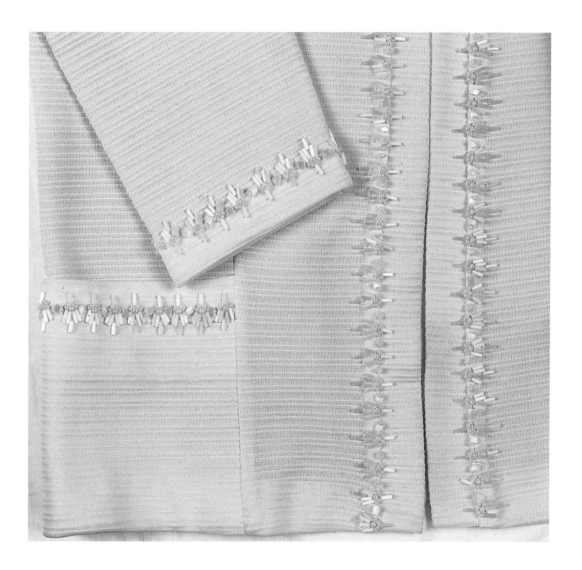

Jersey neckline – Pam Bean

The motif is used to decorate the neckline of a
plain jersey.

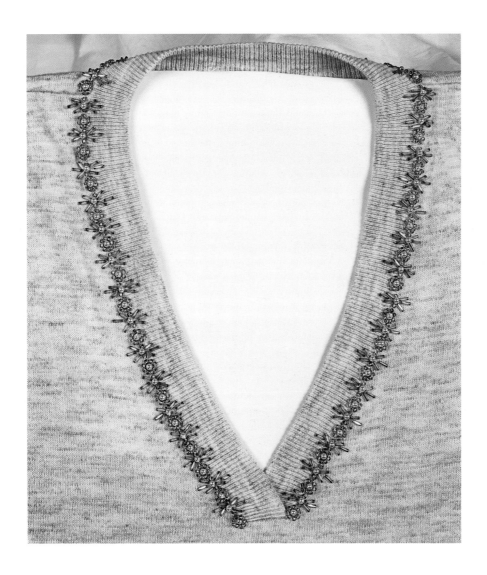

Blouse neckline – Pam Bean

This neckline is worked in cord stitch and oversewing. The flower motifs on the fabric are enhanced with colour-lined beads.

Turquoise spray – Kay Neaves

This spray was designed to echo a marcasite
bow-shaped brooch worn on the dress.

Dress neckline – Kay Neaves

Motifs make up this neckline border, filled with
looped running stitch. The top edge is oversewn, the
lower one is cord stitch.

Shawl – Kay Kelly

This black lace shawl includes silk embroidery.

Gold-lace shawl – Kay Kelly

Cardigan – Louise Jourdain

The embroidery on this cardigan front is loosely
based on cord stitch.

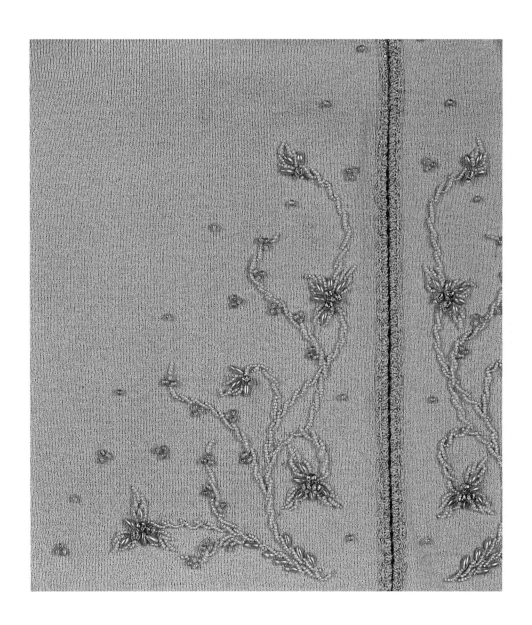

Gold collar with cuffs – Joy Way

Embroidered with whip, stab and running stitches.

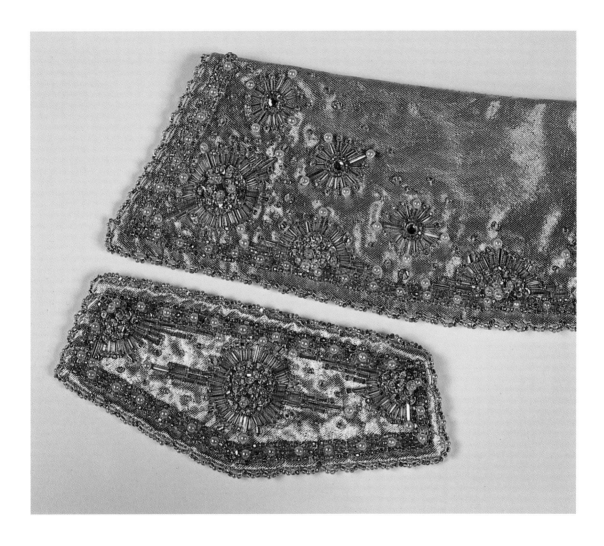

Useful Addresses

The Bead Society of Great Britain
1 Casburn Lane
Burwell
Cambridge
CB5 0ED
Tel/Fax: 01638 742024
www.beadsociety.freeserve.co.uk
A subscription-based, non-profit making organization. The Society holds lectures/workshops, an AGM and an annual Bead Fair. Members also receive five newsletters per year. For a membership form, send a self-addressed envelope to The Secretary at the above address or log onto the website to print one.

The Bead-Workers Guild
PO Box 24922
London
SE23 3WS
Tel: 0870 200 1250
Website: www.beadworkersguild.org.uk

Suppliers

UK

Creative Beadcraft Ltd
Denmark Works
Beamond End
Near Amersham
Bucks
HP7 0RX
Tel: 01494 718510

Ells and Farrier
20 Beak Street
London
W1R 3HA
Tel: 020 7629 9964

Rocking Rabbit
226A High Street
Cottenham
Cambridge
CB4 8RZ
Tel: 0870 606 1588
Email: sales@rockingrabbit.co.uk

Panduro Hobby
Westway House
Transport Avenue
Brentford
Middlesex
TW8 9HF
Customer Services: 020 8847 6161
Website: www.panduro.co.uk

USA

The Bead Shop
899 South Coast Highway
Laguna Beach
CA 92651
Tel: 714 494 2115
Fax 714 494 0380

Bead Box
309 N. Kings Road
Los Angeles
CA 90048
Tel: 213 651 3595
Fax 818 342 3940

Darice
Main Office
13000 Darice Parkway
Park 82
Strongsville
Ohio 44136 6699
Website: www.darice.com

Glossary

Backstitch

Used to sew beads in an unbroken line. The needle has to pass through the last bead of the stitch just completed before threading up the beads for the next one.

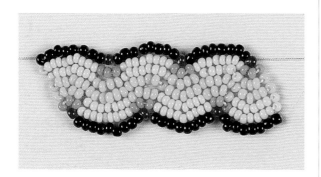

Bead

A general term which takes in all shapes and sizes, though in the exercises within this book, 'beads' refers to embroidery beads. These are usually round, sometimes slightly flattened and are available in many sizes.

Beeswax

A natural wax which helps prevent thread from tangling, fraying or snapping, due to repeatedly passing through the beads.

Bugle

Tube-shaped beads available in many lengths, colours and finishes.

Cord stitch

This is a twisted stitch made to look like a cord and can be used to cover a seam, as an edging, or to give weight to part of a design.

Cut-out motifs

A piece of embroidery cut free from the fabric it is worked on, which can then be attached to another article, such as a garment, belt or other accessory.

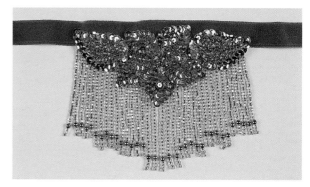

Dressmakers' tracing (carbon) paper

Used by dressmakers and embroiderers to transfer a pattern on to fabric. The marks can be washed out but it is not advisable to wash some beadwork, so all lines need to be covered. Follow manufacturers' instructions.

French chalk (tracing powder)

Can be used to transfer a design onto fabric. Obtainable from a needlwork store, or you can make your own from tailor's chalk, powdered cuttlefish or pumice powder.

Lattice lacing

Decorative technique with a criss-cross lattice appearance. Can look very effective on an evening bag, for example.

Looped fringes

Formed from a sequence of loops – can be a simple, even pattern, or with alternating loop sizes and/or colours.

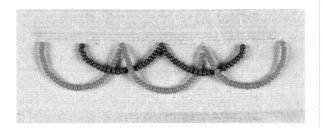

Motif

A design that can be used on its own, scattered or repeated to form a border.

Oversew stitch

Used to enhance an edge.

Pearl

Embroidery pearls are available in round, pear and oval shapes. The core is usually a form of plastic covered with a pearlized finish.

Pouncing

The art or practice of transferring a design by means of pounce.

Pouncing powder

Powder used to transfer a design onto fabric.

Rosette motif

A small flower shaped design, which can be made with beads, sequins or a combination of both. It can be used scattered, placed together in groups or to make borders.

Running stitch

Straight stitches in a line. used to hold beads and sequins in place, with the stitch on the underside of the fabric regulating the space. Used to form borders, to form solid shapes and for outlining. The most versatile stitch as it can be used to embroider a complete garment.

Satin stitch

Stitches laid side by side to fill a solid shape. In this book, beads and bugles are used.

Seeding

An effect created by securing beads, bugles or sequins, using short, straight stitches scattered at various angles.

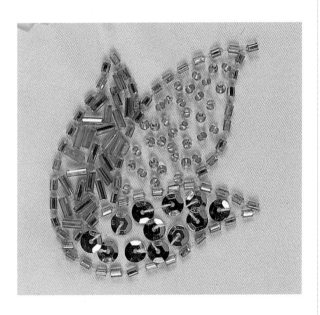

Sequin

Made from very thin plastic material sometimes coated to look like metal, but can also be transparent. Many colours, shapes and sizes are available, including round, square, oval, star, flower and leaf.

Stab stitch

The needle goes back through the fabric at the same point from which it emerged. Very useful for sewing on sequins for scattering, lines and fringes.

Stamen stitch

Used to create flower centres and is based on stab stitch.

Transfer pencil

Used to draw a design in reverse which is then ironed on to fabric. Make sure all lines are covered. It is not always advisable to wash beaded items. Follow manufacturers' instructions.

Vanishing marking pencil

Used to draw a design straight onto fabric.

Whip stitch

A diagonal stitch which can be used in straight and curved lines. Very useful for covering seams.

Zigzag running stitch

Can be used for borders, stripes, curves and so on. Usually worked between two lines.

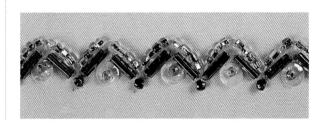

Metric conversion chart

Inches to millimetres

in	mm	in	mm	in	mm	in	mm
1/64	0.3969	41/64	16.2719	1 17/32	38.8938	2 25/32	70.6439
1/32	0.7937	21/32	16.6687	1 9/16	39.6876	2 13/16	71.4376
3/64	1.1906	43/64	17.0656	1 19/32	40.4813	2 27/32	72.2314
1/16	1.5875	11/16	17.4625	1 5/8	41.2751	2 7/8	73.0251
5/64	1.9844	45/64	17.8594	1 21/32	42.0688	2 29/32	73.8189
3/32	2.3812	23/32	18.2562	1 11/16	42.8626	2 15/16	74.6126
7/64	2.7781	47/64	18.6531	1 23/32	43.6563	2 31/32	75.4064
1/8	3.1750	3/4	19.0500	1 3/4	44.4501	3	76.2002
9/64	3.5719	49/64	19.4469	1 25/32	45.2438	3 1/32	76.9939
5/32	3.9687	25/32	19.8437	1 13/16	46.0376	3 1/16	77.7877
11/64	4.3656	51/64	20.2406	1 27/32	46.8313	3 3/32	78.5814
3/16	4.7625	13/16	20.6375	1 7/8	47.6251	3 1/8	79.3752
13/64	5.1594	53/64	21.0344	1 29/32	48.4188	3 5/32	80.1689
7/32	5.5562	27/32	21.4312	1 15/16	49.2126	3 3/16	80.9627
15/64	5.9531	55/64	21.8281	1 31/32	50.0063	3 7/32	81.7564
1/4	6.3500	7/8	22.2250	2	50.8001	3 1/4	82.5502
17/64	6.7469	57/64	22.6219	2 1/32	51.5939	3 9/32	83.3439
9/32	7.1437	29/32	23.0187	2 1/16	52.3876	3 5/16	84.1377
19/64	7.5406	59/64	23.4156	2 3/32	53.1814	3 11/32	84.9314
5/16	7.9375	15/16	23.8125	2 1/8	53.9751	3 3/8	85.7252
21/64	8.3344	61/64	24.2094	2 5/32	54.7688	3 13/32	86.5189
11/32	8.7312	31/32	24.6062	2 3/16	55.5626	3 7/16	87.3127
23/64	9.1281	63/64	25.0031	2 7/32	56.3564	3 15/32	88.1064
3/8	9.5250	1	25.4001	2 1/4	57.1501	3 1/2	88.9002
25/64	9.9219	1 1/32	26.1938	2 9/32	57.9439	3 17/32	89.6939
13/32	10.3187	1 1/16	26.9876	2 5/16	58.7376	3 9/16	90.4877
27/64	10.7156	1 3/32	27.7813	2 11/32	59.5314	3 19/32	91.2814
7/16	11.1125	1 1/8	28.5751	2 3/8	60.3251	3 5/8	92.0752
29/64	11.5094	1 5/32	29.3688	2 13/32	61.1189	3 21/32	92.8689
15/32	11.9062	1 3/16	30.1626	2 7/16	61.9126	3 11/16	93.6627
31/64	12.3031	1 7/32	30.9563	2 15/32	62.7064	3 23/32	94.4564
1/2	12.7000	1 1/4	31.7501	2 1/2	63.5001	3 3/4	95.2502
33/64	13.0969	1 9/32	32.5438	2 17/32	64.2939	3 25/32	96.0439
17/32	13.4937	1 5/16	33.3376	2 9/16	65.0876	3 13/16	96.8377
35/64	13.8906	1 11/32	34.1313	2 19/32	65.8814	3 27/32	97.6314
9/16	14.2875	1 3/8	34.9251	2 5/8	66.6751	3 7/8	98.4252
37/64	14.6844	1 13/32	35.7188	2 21/32	67.4689	3 29/32	99.2189
19/32	15.0812	1 7/16	36.5126	2 11/16	68.2626	3 15/16	100.013
39/64	15.4781	1 15/32	37.3063	2 23/32	69.0564	3 31/32	100.806
5/8	15.8750	1 1/2	38.1001	2 3/4	69.8501	4	101.500

About the Author

Stanley Levy's interest in beadwork started during World War Two. His parents and their families were all clothing manufacturers, and his sister taught him beadwork in the shelters. Upon leaving school he had a desire to become a pastry cook, but at that time was allergic to icing sugar, so went into his parents; gown factory and trained as a machine embroiderer.

To add to Stanley's interests, he was also an amateur ice skater, so was able to combine his skills to decorate a skating dress for his partner with bead embroidery. This led to him beading the dresses of many skaters in the British and World Ice Figure Skating Championships. Stanley's highly regarded work has also included an evening dress for the singer, Frankie Vaughan's wife to wear to a charity function, and costumes for dancers in 'Kismet'.

Upon, the closure of his parents' factory, Stanley took up professional ice skating, and subsequently trained as a florist. While running his own business, he also taught flower arranging in adult education. After six years he sold his business and moved away from London, though continued to teach flower arranging. This led to him starting classes in bead embroidery, and teaching and giving demonstrations to branches of the Women's Institute and Embroiderers' Guild across the south east of England.

Having qualified as a teacher for the City and Guilds Further Education scheme, Stanley regularly gave lectures and demonstrations to other teachers of the courses, showing them teaching techniques. He is a founder member of the Bead Society of Great Britain, and was the first to give a demonstration for them. In addition he has taught bead embroidery in Los Angeles and The Netherlands.

While teaching, Stanley returned to cake decorating, and completed a City and Guilds cake-decorating course, another subject which he has had experience of teaching.

Having been retired in recent years, Stanley has concentrated on writing this bead embroidery book.

Index

A

abbreviations 24

B

backing fabric 65
backstitch 38, 114
  beads 34
    round a pearl 34, 35
    sequins 33, 65
backstitch filling 80
bead oddments 78
beading needles 11
  threading 18
beads 11, 114
  backstitch 34
  finishes 12
  materials 12
  oversew stitch 37
  running stitch 26
  sizes 12–13
  whip stitch 36–7
  with sequins 29
Bean, Pam 99, 105
beeswax 114
belt 78–9
berry motif 44
bleaching beads 17
blood spots 11
blouse neckline 106
blue velvet handbag (McGill) 103
bodice shoulder 84
bodice with pattern 76–7
borders 41, 56, 66, 115, 116

C

box lid or container 17, 20, 22
broken necklaces 78
brooch 65
bugles 11–12, 114
  materials 12
  running stitch 25–6
  sizes 13
  zigzag stitch 42
bunching 26, 27
butterfly collar (Way) 101

cardigan (Jourdain) 111
chequered effect 30, 31
choker 65
clamping stones 51
cleaning beaded items 17
collar 37
colour effects 29, 43, 116
colour fastness 12
colour lined beads 12, 70, 106
  care of 17
contrasting thread 24
cord stitch 49, 106, 108, 111, 114
couching 42, 90
creative embroidery 11, 17, 53, 68, 74
cup sequins 14
curves 26, 34, 37, 41, 43, 116
cut-out motifs 33, 65–6, 84–7, 114

D

daisy petal motif 45–6
diamond shapes 41
dragon motifs 34, 35
dress neckline 108
dressmakers' tracing (carbon) paper 61–2, 114

TITLES AVAILABLE FROM
GMC Publications

BOOKS

WOODCARVING

Beginning Woodcarving	*GMC Publications*
Carving Architectural Detail in Wood:	
The Classical Tradition	*Frederick Wilbur*
Carving Birds & Beasts	*GMC Publications*
Carving Classical Styles in Wood	*Frederick Wilbur*
Carving the Human Figure: Studies in Wood and Stone	*Dick Onians*
Carving Nature: Wildlife Studies in Wood	*Frank Fox-Wilson*
Celtic Carved Lovespoons: 30 Patterns	*Sharon Littley & Clive Griffin*
Decorative Woodcarving (New Edition)	*Jeremy Williams*
Elements of Woodcarving	*Chris Pye*
Figure Carving in Wood: Human and Animal Forms	*Sara Wilkinson*
Lettercarving in Wood: A Practical Course	*Chris Pye*
Relief Carving in Wood: A Practical Introduction	*Chris Pye*
Woodcarving for Beginners	*GMC Publications*
Woodcarving Made Easy	*Cynthia Rogers*
Woodcarving Tools, Materials & Equipment	
(New Edition in 2 vols.)	*Chris Pye*

WOODTURNING

Bowl Turning Techniques Masterclass	*Tony Boase*
Chris Child's Projects for Woodturners	*Chris Child*
Decorating Turned Wood: The Maker's Eye	*Liz & Michael O'Donnell*
Green Woodwork	*Mike Abbott*
A Guide to Work-Holding on the Lathe	*Fred Holder*
Keith Rowley's Woodturning Projects	*Keith Rowley*
Making Screw Threads in Wood	*Fred Holder*
Segmented Turning: A Complete Guide	*Ron Hampton*
Turned Boxes: 50 Designs	*Chris Stott*
Turning Green Wood	*Michael O'Donnell*
Turning Pens and Pencils	*Kip Christensen & Rex Burningham*
Wood for Woodturners	*Mark Baker*
Woodturning: Forms and Materials	*John Hunnex*
Woodturning: A Foundation Course (New Edition)	*Keith Rowley*
Woodturning: A Fresh Approach	*Robert Chapman*
Woodturning: An Individual Approach	*Dave Regester*

Woodturning: A Source Book of Shapes	*John Hunnex*
Woodturning Masterclass	*Tony Boase*
Woodturning Projects: A Workshop Guide to Shapes	*Mark Baker*

WOODWORKING

Beginning Picture Marquetry	*Lawrence Threadgold*
Carcass Furniture	*GMC Publications*
Celtic Carved Lovespoons: 30 Patterns	*Sharon Littley & Clive Griffin*
Celtic Woodcraft	*Glenda Bennett*
Celtic Woodworking Projects	*Glenda Bennett*
Complete Woodfinishing (Revised Edition)	*Ian Hosker*
David Charlesworth's Furniture-Making Techniques	*David Charlesworth*
David Charlesworth's Furniture-Making Techniques	
– Volume 2	*David Charlesworth*
Furniture Projects with the Router	*Kevin Ley*
Furniture Restoration (Practical Crafts)	*Kevin Jan Bonner*
Furniture Restoration: A Professional at Work	*John Lloyd*
Furniture Workshop	*Kevin Ley*
Green Woodwork	*Mike Abbott*
History of Furniture: Ancient to 1900	*Michael Huntley*
Intarsia: 30 Patterns for the Scrollsaw	*John Everett*
Making Heirloom Boxes	*Peter Lloyd*
Making Screw Threads in Wood	*Fred Holder*
Making Woodwork Aids and Devices	*Robert Wearing*
Mastering the Router	*Ron Fox*
Pine Furniture Projects for the Home	*Dave Mackenzie*
Router Magic: Jigs, Fixtures and Tricks to	
Unleash your Router's Full Potential	*Bill Hylton*
Router Projects for the Home	*GMC Publications*
Router Tips & Techniques	*Robert Wearing*
Routing: A Workshop Handbook	*Anthony Bailey*
Routing for Beginners (Revised and Expanded Edition)	*Anthony Bailey*
Stickmaking: A Complete Course	*Andrew Jones & Clive George*
Stickmaking Handbook	*Andrew Jones & Clive George*
Storage Projects for the Router	*GMC Publications*
Success with Sharpening	*Ralph Laughton*

GARDENING

PHOTOGRAPHY

Professional Landscape and Environmental Photography:
  From 35mm to Large Format   *Mark Lucock*
Rangefinder   *Roger Hicks & Frances Schultz*
Underwater Photography   *Paul Kay*
Where and How to Photograph Wildlife   *Peter Evans*
Wildlife Photography Workshops   *Steve & Ann Toon*

Art Techniques

Beginning Watercolours   *Bee Morrison*
Oil Paintings from the Landscape: A Guide for Beginners   *Rachel Shirley*
Oil Paintings from your Garden: A Guide for Beginners   *Rachel Shirley*
Sketching Landscapes in Pen and Pencil   *Joyce Percival*

VIDEOS

Drop-in and Pinstuffed Seats   *David James*   Twists and Advanced Turning   *Dennis White*
Stuffover Upholstery   *David James*   Sharpening the Professional Way   *Jim Kingshott*
Elliptical Turning   *David Springett*   Sharpening Turning & Carving Tools   *Jim Kingshott*
Woodturning Wizardry   *David Springett*   Bowl Turning   *John Jordan*
Turning Between Centres: The Basics   *Dennis White*   Hollow Turning   *John Jordan*
Turning Bowls   *Dennis White*   Woodturning: A Foundation Course   *Keith Rowley*
Boxes, Goblets and Screw Threads   *Dennis White*   Carving a Figure: The Female Form   *Ray Gonzalez*
Novelties and Projects   *Dennis White*   The Router: A Beginner's Guide   *Alan Goodsell*
Classic Profiles   *Dennis White*   The Scroll Saw: A Beginner's Guide   *John Burke*

MAGAZINES

WOODTURNING ◆ WOODCARVING
FURNITURE & CABINETMAKING ◆ THE ROUTER
NEW WOODWORKING ◆ THE DOLLS' HOUSE MAGAZINE
OUTDOOR PHOTOGRAPHY ◆ BLACK & WHITE PHOTOGRAPHY
KNITTING ◆ GUILD NEWS

The above represents a full list of all titles currently published or scheduled to be published.
All are available direct from the Publishers or through bookshops, newsagents and specialist retailers.
To place an order, or to obtain a complete catalogue, contact:

GMC Publications,
Castle Place, 166 High Street, Lewes, East Sussex BN7 1XU United Kingdom
Tel: 01273 488005 Fax: 01273 402866
E-mail: pubs@thegmcgroup.com
Website: www.gmcbooks.com

Orders by credit card are accepted

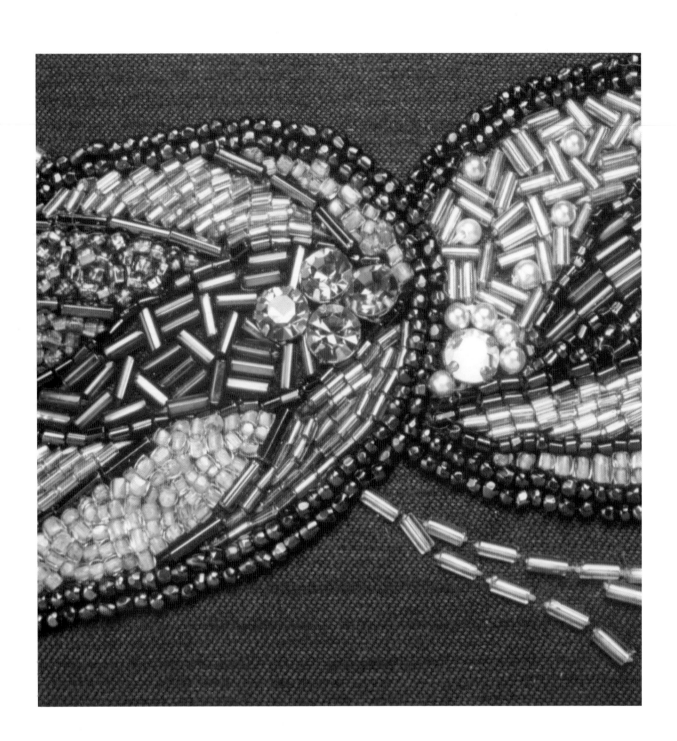